STORIES OF MUSLIM WOMEN

QUARRY
WOMEN'S
BOOKS

Reading Rights: A Women's Guide to the Law in Canada
by RAHAT KURD

Siolence: Poets on Women, Violence & Silence
Edited by SUSAN MCMASTER

Arguments with the World: Essays by Bronwen Wallace
Edited by JOANNE PAGE

Woman of Sticks, Woman of Stones
by SANDRA NICHOLLS

Dangerous Elements
by SARAH KLASSEN

At My Mother's Feet

STORIES OF MUSLIM WOMEN

Edited by
SADIA ZAMAN

FOR THE CANADIAN COUNCIL OF MUSLIM WOMEN

QUARRY
WOMEN'S
BOOKS

The publisher gratefully acknowledges the support of
the Book Publishing Industry Development Program
of the Department of Canadian Heritage.

The Canadian Council of Muslim Women gratefully
acknowledge the support of the Department of Canadian Heritage
(Multiculturalism) and Status of Women (Women's Program).

ISBN 1-55082-263-2

Cover photograph of Rikia Haidar, courtesy of Aliya Mohammed Ali.

Design by Susan Hannah.

Printed and bound in Canada by AGMV Marquis,
Cap-Saint-Ignace, Québec.

Published by Quarry Press Inc.,
P.O. Box 1061, Kingston,
Ontario K7L 4Y5 Canada,
www.quarrypress.com

Contents

At My Mother's Feet

A man came to the Prophet and said,
"O Messenger of Allah I intend to go
on an (military) expedition, but I've
come to ask for your advice.
    The Prophet asked,
    "Is your mother alive?"
    The man replied, "Yes."
    The Prophet said,
    "Then stay with her,
for the Garden is under her feet."

Hadith as reported by Ibn Majah and al-Nasa'i

Introduction

I never knew my mother's mother. She died suddenly when my mother was 17, three days after my mother had received her high school transcripts. My grandmother had been making the financial preparations to send her daughter to college. This was no small task as my grandfather did not believe young women needed an education. However, my grandmother was determined. She was a practical woman who believed that an education would secure a better future for her daughter. Even though my grandmother was an extremely devout Muslim, it was the same sense of practicality that allowed her to hide a pregnant teenager in her home for a week while the girl's mother arranged for an abortion. Abortions were illegal in Pakistan. There is no written record of this strong woman, this pioneer. The few stories I have are filtered through my mother's memories.

My mother did get her college education and eventually married my father. After seven years of marriage, she left not only the security of her extended family, but also the Pakistani culture that had nurtured her, to join my father in Denmark. With five children and little money, she worked in a chocolate factory during the day and came home to an even more demanding shift. She adapted to a different language and culture, and in the process saw the erosion of her own. We, her children, were embarrassed at how different we were from our classmates so we spoke Danish most of the time. It would get much worse when we moved to Canada to a new language and yet another culture. My parents chased the immigrant dream of a good education for their children. But it was an elusive goal, one that included financial hardship, and a cold winter in a Saskatchewan trailer court. It was not the life my mother had imagined. So through the constant readjustment of her expectations and the daily process of survival, she too was forced to adopt the spirit of a pioneer.

My family was the only Muslim family in the small prairie town that eventually became home. I spent most of my school years hoping no one would notice I was different. But it didn't work. School was a series of painful incidents familiar to any child who has been an outsider. In grade five my teacher hauled me in front of the class because I didn't sing the national anthem. Since I wouldn't sing with the rest of the class, she decided I should do it in front of the class. The problem was, I didn't know the words. My family had only been in Canada six months and my English was not great. So there I stood for a lifetime, humiliated in front of my peers.

On special occasions my family drove an hour to the mosque in Saskatoon. I didn't really fit in with the kids there; they were city people and seemed much more sophisticated. There were only two girls who were my age, and we had nothing in common. When I finished high school, I desperately wanted to study journalism, but no woman in that community had ever done such a thing. Journalism was not part of the collective dream of parents who had sacrificed everything so their children would never have it as tough as they did. When a child became a doctor, a lawyer, or an engineer, it eased the minds of parents who were exhausted from chasing the immigrant dream. Besides, journalism, especially television journalism, was considered an immodest profession for a woman. The stereotypical image of a reporter shoving a microphone in some politician's face, chasing stories day and night, did not go over well in a community that was proud of its modesty.

The truth was, no one really knew what one did with a journalism degree. I wasn't really sure myself. I had never met or seen a journalist who was not white, let alone one from a Muslim background. All I knew was that I wanted to tell stories. And I have — stories of all kinds of strong women, often women who've never had a public voice. I've had the immense pleasure of travelling across this great country while working with the Canadian Broadcasting Corporation as well as private broadcasters. I now work with Vision TV, a national non-profit network that is devoted to telling stories about moral, ethical, and spiritual issues.

In 1992 I travelled to South Africa to do a series of documentaries for Vision TV. In a squatter camp near Johannesburg, a Muslim woman risked her life, her standing in her upper-class community, and her personal relationships to help feed black children. Her sense of social justice was humbling. It wasn't until that story aired that I realized that I had never seen such a strong, defiant Muslim woman on the screen. The media obsession with Muslim women as victims of their faith and cultures leaves little room for other images.

In 1995, while official delegates met at the United Nations Forum on Women in Beijing, other women from non-governmental organizations were bussed to the small city of Huairou for their own forum. In front of the main conference building, a woman screamed and threw paper balls at another woman trapped in a box. This was a mock stoning, a protest against Islamic leaders who incite followers to torture women. One afternoon a woman from Sudan spoke about genital mutilation, of how local religious leaders have appropriated a cultural practice. These leaders tell women it is their religious duty to "cut" their daughters for it will guarantee them a place in heaven. A South African Muslim woman asked me if it is true, that women are really being mutilated and stoned. None of it made sense in the day-to-day Islam that she practices. Yes, I said, it is true. But there are many other truths that rarely make it to the public arena, truths that are not part of our books and our histories.

This book tries to get at some of those other truths through women who have felt excluded from our public history most of their lives. The majority of women I approached were surprised that anyone would care about their early experiences in Canada or about their contributions to their communities. No one had ever asked them to tell their stories, and so they were much too modest about their achievements, and extremely guarded about their challenges. It was a struggle to get women to admit that they'd had any. In my conversations with these women, I found a deeply ingrained modesty as well as a reluctance to speak publicly about painful events. As you read these very personal stories, I hope you will do so with an appreciation of the courage it took some of the women to reveal things that may not be all that surprising in themselves. But coming from women who are often stereotyped and misunderstood, to reveal anything outside of their communities is remarkable.

This book is the brainchild of the Canadian Council of Muslim Women (CCMW). The primary objectives of the organization are to give Canadian Muslim women an understanding of their rights and responsibilities, to strengthen the bonds of sisterhood among diverse Islamic communities, and to contribute to Canadian society. The Council tries to promote Muslim women's identities through its events and projects. It is in this later context that the CCMW wants to record the lives of some of Canada's Muslim women, women pioneers.

The process of putting this book together took two years. CCMW asked its chapters across the country for names of some of the women who should be approached. I tracked down other women through word of mouth. Some of the stories were developed from written submissions, one from an oral submission, and the rest from in-depth interviews. It was Muslim women themselves, who, at the 1997 CCMW conference in London, Ontario, defined the term 'pioneer'. During a workshop about forty women decided a pioneer is someone who creates change, is determined and courageous, is a risk-taker who initiates leadership, is patient and resilient, is driven and balanced, is often an outcast in society yet compassionate, and someone who has a vision of the future.

In the pages to come you'll meet women who possess these qualities. In the first part of the book, you'll meet women who are pioneers in the literal sense. Many of these early Muslim women came to Canada from the Arab world, including Amina and Rikia. Their remarkable journey to this country took them through war, to prairie homesteads, to a new life that included heartbreak over a child left behind in Lebanon. Others, like Lila, were born in Canada and helped create some of the first institutions for Muslim women in the country. Lila also helped save the oldest mosque in North America from demolition. Then you'll meet people like Solmaz, women who came during many waves of immigration in the 1960s and '70s. Solmaz came to Canada out of choice and found that her new life was much more difficult than the one she had left behind. Towards the end of the book, you'll meet pioneers of a different sort, women who use their volunteer activism to improve the lives of Muslim women in Canada and abroad, at some personal cost. One of those women is Mariam, a seventeenth-generation French-Canadian whose drive, courage, and compassion took her to the refugee camps of Croatia.

The stories are told by the women in their own words, though in two cases they are filtered through memories of daughters. They are universal stories about isolation, loneliness, faith, and compassion. The incredible spirit with which these women overcame struggles and embraced challenges is also universal. However, the voices telling the stories are new. Of course, these voices belong to just a few of the thousands of strong, spirited, Muslim women in this country. This book cannot capture all those voices; it is merely an attempt to record the living history of a few of the Muslim women in Canada. Nevertheless, it is a book that is long overdue. The women in this book, as well as everyone on the CCMW executive, worked very hard to help record this history, and they all did it as volunteers. I am so very grateful for their efforts. The Department of Canadian Heritage, Multiculturalism and Status of Women, Canada also supported this project.

I am also indebted to women like Ayshi Hassan and Eva Wahab who could not be part of the book, but, nevertheless, helped me understand the challenges of building community when there are no role models and no institutions to turn to. Ayshi lived through war, raised 11 children, and was one the founders of the vibrant Muslim community in London, Ontario. Further north in Ottawa, Ontario, Eva Wahab formed the Muslim Women's Auxiliary by looking up people with Muslim names in the phone book. She ran her own restaurant, and was part of an exhibition about Canadian Muslims at Expo '67.

My family and friends also contributed to this book

through their encouragement and patience. Alia Hogben was a constant voice of reason. Fellow journalist and friend Ann Rauhala read the manuscript and made wonderful suggestions. My husband also made invaluable contributions to this project. He fixed all the computer glitches, became a messenger service, and kept a very active child busy while her mommy was locked away in the office. Most of all, he encouraged me when I was exhausted and graciously gave up much of his time with me.

What is not recorded does not last in our consciousness, and it does not exist for future generations. As the mother of a daughter, I have a vested interest in fostering a sense of collective history. My daughter's strength will come not only from her great-grandmother, her grandmother, and perhaps her mother, but also from the stories of the Muslim women who helped build this country. So this project is a labor of love, for my daughter, and for all the daughters and sons.

Sadia Zaman

Historical Background

History and society have often relegated Muslim women to the back stage of the world scene into silence and anonymity. If these women are recognized at all, it is often in the context of how they helped their husbands. Where are the accounts — historical, sociological, and statistical — of Muslim women and their achievements in the official records or in the historical and cultural studies? Usually, it is the activities and accomplishments of men that tell the story of Muslims in Canada. This brief historical background will attempt to put some of the Muslim women on the front stage.

Muslim migration to Canada has taken place in phases, depending on world events and the immigration policies of the Canadian government. According to Abu Laban the earliest record of Muslim presence in Canada was found in the 1871 Census of Canada.[1] It recorded 13 Muslims, all males. By 1901 the number was estimated to be between 300-400, and by 1911 it had grown to 1500. These early Muslims came from Greater Syria, which today includes Lebanon, Syria, Palestine, and Jordan. They also came from Turkey, which was ruled by the Ottoman Empire. In fact, around the turn of the century several Muslim immigrants came to North America to escape the conscription in the Turkish army. But by 1931 the Muslim population had decreased to 645 partly because many Turks returned to their homeland during World War I. In North

America they were seen as enemies because of Turkey's support of Germany during the war. At the same time, the Canadian government also began to restrict immigration from Asian countries and this also reduced the number of Muslims in Canada.

Over the next 20 years only 2,000 to 3,000 Muslims resided in Canada. But by 1970, Canadian Encyclopaedia records show the population had grown to 33,370.[2] Statistics Canada records show that between 1970 to 1981 the number of Muslim immigrants increased to 98,160 and then to 253,260 by 1991.[3] At the same time the ethnic composition of these immigrants also changed. As reported in the publication *Muslims in the Canadian Mosaic*, Muslims now came from many more countries: Egypt, Iran, Pakistan, India, Bangladesh, Eastern Europe, East Africa, the Caribbean, Mauritius, Far Eastern countries, the United States and the United Kingdom.[4]

Population Growth of Canadian Muslims

YEARS	ESTIMATED NUMBERS
1871	13
1901	300-400
1911	1500
1931	645
1951	2000-3000
1970	33,370
1981	98,160
1991	253,260

The dramatic increase in the number of Muslims recorded in 1970 can be explained by changes in immigration rules when a quota system was changed to a point system. Before 1970, every country was assigned an arbitrary number of immigrants, and many Asian countries were assigned low quotas. When the system was changed, immigrants were admitted to Canada based on their education, their employment, and their language abilities. This change allowed many immigrants from Muslim countries to enter Canada. The community grew again as many of these new Canadians sponsored their extended families. Then, in the 1980s, many Muslims entered Canada as refugees from places as diverse as Afghanistan, Bosnia, and Somalia.

There was no official record of Muslim women in Canada until the 1980s. For the first time, in the 1981 Census, religious affiliation was recorded by gender and province. So we know that in 1981 there were 45, 535 Muslim women, and a decade later,[5] in the 1991 Census, that number had more than doubled to 115, 365.[6] The majority (67,540) lived in Ontario, followed by a population of 18, 015 in Quebec, while 16,180 Muslim women resided in Alberta. These numbers show only what was recorded in the 1981 Census and 1991 Census. We do not have any records prior to these dates.

Population by Religion and Sex for Canada 1991

RELIGION/SEX

	CANADA	ONTARIO	QUEBEC	ALBERTA	BRITISH COLUMBIA	NOVA SCOTIA
ISLAM	253,260	145,560	44,930	31,000	24,930	1,435
MALES	137,895	78,020	26,910	16,185	12,975	830
FEMALES	115,365	67,540	18,015	11,955	11,955	605

In 1991, 15,060 women were between the ages of 45 and 64, and 4,170 were over the age of 65. We have no way of knowing how many of these women are among the earliest Muslim settlers, or how many are direct descendants of the first Canadian Muslim women. These gaps in the historical information can be filled with material from oral history and biography research.

Age Group of Muslims by Sex 1991

ISLAM	Less than 15 years	15-24 years	25-44	45-64	65 Years and over
TOTAL	71,575	40,000	98,960	35,265	7,735
MALES	36,950	20,995	56,175	20,205	3,570
FEMALES	34,625	19,005	42,510	15,060	4,170

Surely among the first Muslim women to come to Canada was Fatmi Kaziel. Fatmi Kaziel came from Syria in 1912 by boat with her husband. They landed in Newfoundland and eventually took a train to Saskatchewan, where two of her husband's brothers had settled. Her niece, Aishi Kaziel, came with her parents in 1923, first to Saskatchewan then to Alberta. Hilwie Hamdon came to Saskatchewan in 1922 after crossing the ocean on *The Queen Elizabeth*. Dhebie Terrabain came in 1920, Fatmi Shaban came sometime soon after 1914. Miryam Teha told me, through her daughter, that she came with her two daughters in 1930 to Saskatchewan and eventually to Alberta. Some of these women came because their husbands had heard about land in Canada, others came with men who wanted to escape conscription in the Turkish army. But the majority came under social network and family reunion migration categories as their husbands and other relatives were already in Canada. I mention the names of these women deliberately because women often go unnamed or are named only as so-and so's mother or wife.

These early immigrants set up homesteads, built small log cabins or sod houses, and established tiny isolated hamlets. Most of the women settled into farm life and milked cows, churned butter, raised cattle and poultry, and also took care of their families. Aishie Kaziel told me of terrible snowstorms where women had to tie thick ropes from the house to the barn so they would not be blown away by the wind. Lanterns were lit at either end of the ropes to combat total invisibility in the snow, even during the day. There was no running water so ice had to be cut and melted. This ice was stored in the ice houses for summer. Another woman told me that as a child she had ice cream in July, made on those ice slabs. The women cooked not only for their families but also for the hired hands, particularly during harvest. Since money was scarce during the 1920s and '30s, women sold butter and eggs and other farm produce. Often they hired Arab men to teach Arabic to the children.

Aishie Kaziel did not know how to read or write, yet education was very important to her. She came to Edmonton for her children's schooling. An Arab peddler who lived with the family taught the children. Once this peddler acquired a copy of the novel *Gone With the Wind*, and Aishie's husband read it out loud while she listened to the story with rapt attention.

Another pioneer, Hilwie Hamdon lived on a farm in Fort Chipewyan, Alberta. Her granddaughter-in-law described her life on the farm in Fort Chipewyan in the 1920s. She told me the Hamdon family went out to Fort McMurray by dog sled in spring to shop. In summer they travelled by boat. Her grandmother-in-law told her the story of what happened one time when the grandmother was alone in the farmhouse. She saw a face in the window, opened the door, and admitted a Chipewyan Indian into the house. The man was taken aback at her trusting nature and stayed, guarding her until her husband returned. The Indian then showed his disapproval to the husband because he had left his wife alone. Hilwie Hamdon told her granddaughter-in-law that she found the Indians very friendly and often invited them to the house to share a meal. Hilwie Hamdon was a spirited woman who learned to play bridge and taught herself to read the Qur 'an in English even, though she could only spell phonetically.

Another old woman remembered her childhood on the Fort Chipewyan farm where people always got together for food and laughter. This Lebanese-Syrian community consisted of Arab Muslims and Christians who celebrated Eid together. The women of this community built their own support networks and participated in marriages, festivals, and funerals together.

Some of the Muslim families who settled in western Canadian towns bought rooming houses. Miriam Teha's mother worked in a rooming house and her aunt worked in a hotel. The rooming houses charged $.05 a bed a night, with four or five beds in a room. Peddlers who were bachelors stayed in the rooming houses. The women worked hard to establish their businesses and did not get paid. Other Muslim women worked in general stores.

Abu-Laban states that ties with the homeland decreased as the local community became a substitute extended family.[7] When Hilwie Hamdon came to Edmonton in 1932, she joined the Liberal Women's Association of Edmonton and was also a member of the Eastern Star. With some friends she founded The Red Crescent, a branch of the Red Cross, and collected money and knitted for Canadian soldiers. During this period there was far greater integration of Muslim women into the larger society than is usually the case with recent immigrants. This is partly due to the fact that because there were so few of them, Muslim women had no choice but to mix with the larger community. There was not an aggressive need to assert a separate Muslim identity, and Muslim and Christian women often celebrated their holy days together.

These pioneer women were heroic women. They worked hard to sustain their families and to build their communities within an alien culture and language. Through this book we honor these women for their courage, their capacity to work hard, and their ability to meet the challenges of a new world.

Zohra Husaini

Notes

1 Abu Lahan, Baha, "Canadian Muslims: Need for a New Survival Strategy," *Journal of Muslim Minority Affairs*, 1981, p. 48-49.

2 *The Canadian Encycopaedia*, 1985, p. 906.

3 *The Census of Canada* (1981), Population, Religion, Catalogue Number 92-912, Ottawa: Statistics Canada, 1993, p. 14.

4 Husaini, Zohra, *Muslims in the Canadian Mosaic*, Muslim Research Foundation, Edmonton, 1990.

5 *Census of Canada* (1981), op. cit., p. 1-1.

6 *Census of Canada* (1991), op. cit., p. 14.

7 Abu-Laban, Sharon Melvin, "Family and Religion Among Muslim Immigrants and Their Descendants," in ed. Earle H. Waugh et al, op. cit., p. 15.

Sources for Tables

Population Growth of Canadian Muslims, 1991

Data for 1871 to 1951 compiled from Abu-Laban, Baha. "Canadian Muslims: The Need for a New Survival Strategy," Journal: Institute of Muslim Minority Affairs. 1981, p. 98-99.

Data for 1970 compiled from The Canadian Encyclopaedia. Edmonton: Hurtig, 1985, p. 906.

Data for 1981 from Statistics Canada. Census of Canada. Population, Religion. Catalogue 91-912. Ottawa: December 1983, p. 9.

Data for 1991 from *Religions in Canada, The Nation* 1991 Census Statistics Canada Catalogue 93-319, published by authority of Minister Responsible for Statistics Canada, 1993, p. 19

Population by Religion and Sex for Canada, 1991

Compiled from *Religions in Canada, The Nation* 1991 Census, Statistics Canada – Catalogue 93 – 319, published by authority of the Minister Responsible for Statistics Canada, 1993, p. 14.

Age Group of Muslims by Sex

Compiled from *Religions in Canada, The Nation* 1991 Census, Statistics Canada – Catalogue 93-319, published by authority of the Minister Responsible for Statistics Canada, 1993, p. 19.

About Islam

The Arabic word Islam simply means 'submission.' In a religious context, Islam means complete submission to the will of God. Allah is the Arabic name for God, used by Arab Muslims and Christians alike.

Muslims believe in one God; in the Angels created by Him; in the prophets through whom His revelations were brought to mankind; in the Day of Judgement and individual accountability for actions; in God's complete authority over human destiny and in life after death. Muslims believe in a chain of prophets starting with Adam and including Noah, Abraham, Ishmael, Isaac, Jacob, Joseph, Job, Moses, Aaron, David, Solomon, Elias, Jonah, John the Baptist, and Jesus. But God's final message to man was revealed to the Prophet Muhammad through Gabriel. Islam, Christianity, and Judaism all go back to the prophet and patriarch Abraham, and their three prophets are directly descended from his sons — Muhammad from the eldest, Ishmael, and Moses and Jesus from Isaac. Abraham established the settlement which today is the city of Mecca, and built the Ka'ba towards which all Muslims turn when they pray.

Muhammad was born in Mecca in the year 570, at a time when Christianity was not yet fully established in Europe. Since his father died before his birth, and his mother shortly afterwards, he was raised by his uncle from the respected tribe

of Quraysh. As he grew up, he became known for his truthful-
ness, generosity, and sincerity, so that he was sought after for
his ability to arbitrate in disputes. The historians describe him
as calm and meditative.

Muhammad was of a deeply religious nature and had long
detested the decadence of his society. It became his habit to
meditate from time to time in the cave of Hira near the sum-
mit of Jabal al-Nur, the 'Mountain of Light' near Mecca.

At the age of forty, while engaged in a meditative retreat,
Muhammad received his first revelation from God through the
Angel Gabriel. This revelation, which continued for twenty-
three years, is known as the Qur'an. As soon as he began to
recite the words he heard from Gabriel, Muhammad and his
small group of followers suffered bitter persecution, and in the
year 622 God gave them the command to emigrate. This
event, the Hijra (migration), in which they left Mecca for the
city of Madina some 260 miles to the north, marks the beginning of the Muslim calendar. After several years, the Prophet
and his followers were able to return to Mecca, where they for-
gave their enemies and established Islam. Before the Prophet
died at the age of 63, the greater part of Arabia was Muslim,
and within a century of his death Islam had spread to Spain in
the west and as far east as China.

The Qur'an is a record of the exact words revealed by God
through the Angel Gabriel to the Prophet Muhammad. It was
memorized by Muhammad and then dictated to his companions, and written down by scribes, who cross-checked it during
his lifetime. Not one word of its 114 chapters, or suras, has
been changed over the centuries. The Qur'an is the prime
source of every Muslim's faith and practice. It deals with all the
subjects that concern us as human beings: wisdom, doctrine,
worship, and law, but its basic theme is the relationship between
God and His creatures. The Qur'an also provides guidelines for
a just society, proper human conduct, and an equitable eco-
nomic system.

The Muslim population of the world is around one billion.
Thirty per cent of Muslims live in the Indian subcontinent,

twenty percent in Sub-Saharan Africa, seventeen percent in Southeast Asia, eighteen percent in the Arab world, ten percent in the Soviet Union and China. There are Muslim minorities in almost every area of the world, including Latin America and Australia, while the world's largest Muslim community is in Indonesia.

The Five Pillars of Islam

Faith

There is no God worthy of worship except God and Muhammad is His messenger. This declaration of faith is called the Shahada, a simple formula that all the faithful pronounce in Arabic.

Prayer

Salat is the name for the obligatory prayers, which are performed five times a day, and are a direct link between the worshipper and God. There is no hierarchical authority in Islam, and no priests, so the prayers are led by a learned person who knows the Qur'an and is chosen by the congregation. These five prayers contain verses from the Qur'an, and are said in Arabic, the language of the Revelation, but personal supplication can be offered in one's own language.

Prayers are said at dawn, noon, mid-afternoon, sunset and nightfall, and determine the rhythm of the entire day. Although it is preferable for Muslims to worship together in a mosque, Muslims may pray almost anywhere. The prayer can be translated as 'God is most great. God is most great. God is most great. God is most great. I testify that there is no god except God. I testify that there is no god except God. I testify that Muhammad is the messenger of God. I testify that Muhammad is the messenger of God. Come to prayer! Come to prayer! Come to success (in this life and the Hereafter)! Come to success! God is most great. God is most great. There is no god except God.' Once Muslims prayed towards Jerusalem, but during the Prophet's lifetime it was changed to Mecca.

Zakat

One of the most important principles of Islam is that all things belong to God, and that wealth is therefore held by human beings in trust. The word zakat means both 'purification' and 'growth'. Possessions are purified by setting aside a proportion for those in need. Each Muslim calculates his or her own zakat individually. For most purposes this involves the payment of two-and-a-half percent of one's capital every year.

The Fast

Every year in the month of Ramadan, all Muslims fast from first light until sundown, abstaining from food, drink, and sexual relations. Those who are sick, elderly, or on a journey, and women who are pregnant or nursing are permitted to break the fast and make up an equal number of days later in the year. If that is not possible, they must feed a needy person for every day missed. Children begin to fast (and to observe the prayer) from puberty, although many start earlier.

The Pilgrimage (Hajj)

The annual pilgrimage to Mecca, the Hajj, is an obligation only for those who are physically and financially able to perform it. About two million people go to Mecca each year from every comer of the globe; the annual Hajj begins in the twelfth month of the Islamic year (which is lunar, not solar, so that Hajj and Ramadan can fall either in summer or winter). Pilgrims wear special clothes: simple garments, which strip away distinctions of class and culture, so that all stand equal before God. The rites of the Hajj, which are of Abrahamic origin, include circling the Ka'ba seven times, and going seven times between the mountains of Safa and Marwa as did Hagar during her search for water. Then the pilgrims stand together on the wide plain of Arafa and join in prayers for God's forgiveness, in what is often thought of as a preview to the Last Judgement. The close of the Hajj is marked by a festival, Eid al-Adhha, which is celebrated with prayers and the exchange of gifts.

Glossary of Terms

Eid

The word Eid is an Arabic term for a festivity, a celebration, a recurring happiness, and a feast. In Islam, there are two major Eids, the feast of Ramadan (Eid Al-Fitr) and the Feast of Sacrifice (Eid Al-Adhha). The first Eid is celebrated by Muslims after fasting the month of Ramadan. It takes place on the first day of Shawwal, the tenth month of the lunar calendar. The second Eid is the Feast of Sacrifice and it is celebrated in memory of prophet Ibrahim's willingness to sacrifice his son Isma'il. This Eid lasts four days between the tenth and the thirteenth day of Zul-Hijjah, the twelfth month of the lunar calendar.

Hajj

Hajj is the performance of pilgrimage to Mecca. A Muslim is to perform Hajj at least once in his/her life, if means and health allow. Hajj takes place during the last month of the lunar calendar called the month of Zul-Hijjah.

Halal

Halal is something that is lawful and permitted in Islam. Often the term refers to meat from an animal that has been slaughtered according to Islamic guidelines.

Imam

An imam is a religious leader. Any person who leads a congregational prayer is called an imam. A religious leader who also leads his community in the political affairs may be called an imam, an amir, or a caliph. However, an imam is not infallible. He is responsible for his mistakes to all the members of the community and above all he is responsible to Allah.

Ka'ba

The first house of worship built for mankind. It was originally built by Adam and later on reconstructed by Abraham and Isma'il. It is a cube-shaped structure in the city of Mecca to which all Muslims turn in their five daily prayers.

Lunar Calendar

In their religious duties, Muslims depend on solar and lunar calendars. The latter is shorter than the solar by twelve days. Fasting during the month of Ramadan, celebrating the two major feasts (Eid Al-Fitr and Eid Al-Adhha), performing the pilgrimage to Mecca, and other religious activities depend upon the lunar months. The names of the lunar months are: Maharrem, Safar, Rabi' Al-Awwal, Rabi' Al-Akhar, Jamada Al-Akhirah, Rajab, Sha'ban, Ramadan, Shawwal, Zul-Qi'dah, and Zul-Hijjah. The timing of the daily prayers depend on the solar system.

Ramadan

The holy month of prescribed fasting for Muslims. It was during this month that the Qur'anic revelations began.

The above information was compiled from the ISL Software Corporation web site at www.islsoftware.com. *The material is being used in this book with permission from the creators of the web site.*

Amina & Rikia

The story of my grandmother Amina and mother Rikia and their journey to Canada began in the Bekaa Valley in the village of Marj early in the twentieth century. Lebanon, then part of Syria, was under the domination of the Ottoman Empire. The valley had fertile fruit orchards, vegetable gardens, and grain farms situated between two mountain ranges. The eastern boundary formed the shores of the Mediterranean. Beirut, the capital, was an important port on the trade routes for the country's seafarers, descendants of the Phoenicians.

Many young men left the Bekaa Valley to seek adventure and fortune in the new world, and among them were Amina's brothers. The only sister of Salim, Hassan and Abdul Karim Shaben, Amina had been widowed early with two daughters — Rikia, born in 1905, and Zainab, a year later. Amina was very close to her brothers, and when they settled in the United States, they invited her for a six-month visit.

Amina was persuaded by her father to leave her daughter Zainab, then five, with him and she reluctantly agreed — a decision she regretted as the ship left the port of Beirut. Rikia watched her mother weep all the way to Marseilles. They missed the connecting ship to New York because Amina's eyes were so inflamed from crying that the health authorities feared an infection and detained mother and daughter. The next ship to New York had a scheduled stop in Vera Cruz, Mexico, and the timing of Amina and Rikia's arrival was most unfortunate.

Amina Haidar (left)
and her daughter Rikia 1949.

In May of 1911, Mexican President Porfiro Diaz was over-thrown by Francisco Madero who became president and ignit-ed a revolution. The revolution had reduced the country to a state of chaos. Mexican leaders Victoriano Heurta, Francisco Villa, Eulatio Guttierrez and Venustiano Carranza held various areas of the country and were fighting each other.

Amina and Rikia's ship was confiscated in Vera Cruz and all passengers were forced to disembark. In all the chaos, trav-el to the United States was impossible. The trains were stopped in search of men seeking to avoid military service. There was looting of trains and mass slaughter of men, women, and chil-dren. Amina and Rikia had no choice but to remain in Mexico City. They stayed with families from the Bekaa Valley, and as time passed and funds were depleted, Amina joined other women in baking Arab bread to make a living. Rikia went to school and learned Spanish, including the lullabies she would one day sing to her children. The nuns in her school found her name difficult and their version of Rikia became Maria, then Mary — a name that was to remain with her throughout her life.

Nearly five years passed before Amina and Rikia could leave safely for the border town of Loredo, Texas, where Amina's brothers met them. During those years, Amina could not communicate with her father, and no ships arrived from the Bekaa with news of her father and Zainab. It was 1915 and mother and daughter accompanied Amina's brothers to Sioux City, Iowa, then Calgary, and finally to Edmonton, where Rikia attended school.

The First World War was in progress. Hussein Sherif of Mecca agreed to aid the allied war effort by organizing the Arab revolt against the Ottomans (led by Lawrence of Arabia) in return for Arab independence. It was a promise that was not honored. The war raged throughout the Middle East, includ-ing the Bekaa Valley.

News filtered out of Marj, Amina's village in the Bekaa, that Amina's father had died in the war. No one could provide any information on Zainab's whereabouts. Amina was told that her youngest daughter had perished along with many others. She could not accept this and continued to search. She heard a rumor that on the day the local Turkish governor fled to

Turkey with his family, Zainab had been playing with his children. The Red Crescent was asked to search in Turkey for Zainab and requests were made through diplomatic channels. None of Amina's efforts were successful, and she spent the rest of her life mourning for a daughter she could not find. She rarely spoke of this tragedy, but through the years we would listen outside the closed bedroom door to our grandmother's heartbreaking lament, asking for Zainab's forgiveness.

Our father Mahmoud's adventures began in another part of the Bekaa in the village of Jib Jenine. Perched on the side of a mountain range, overlooking the beautiful valley, the sprinkling of lights of the many small towns strung along the face of the opposite mountain lit up the night sky. In 1900, at the age of 17, Mahmoud left this beautiful home for the United States. He never returned.

Father's love of the land began in the family orchards and farms in the Bekaa and followed him to his new world as he worked his way from Ellis Island, New York, through the farmlands to his first homestead in Saskatchewan. At the Canadian border he was asked his name — Mahmoud Saeed el Haj Ahmed Abi Lamah. The appalled immigration officer recorded the first two names only, Mahmoud Saeed. The Saeed became Saddy. El Haj Ahmed, his grandfather's name and Abi Lamah, the family names were gone. In those days Mahmoud was a strange name, so he was called Big Sam, and because the Arabs were considered Turks and enemies of Britain in the First War, my father was also called the "Turk." It was his first experience with racial prejudice.

Mahmoud was joined in Saskatchewan by his brother Ali, and together they expanded their homestead into a successful farming operation. In 1920 Ali returned to Lebanon to look after family property, and besides, he was homesick. He wanted Mahmoud to go with him to get married 'back home'. Before leaving for Jib Jenine with his brother, Mahmoud went to Alberta to check out some farmland. It was there he met Rikia. He, tall and handsome, and she, a petite, blue-eyed beauty, fell in love.

Mahmoud and Rikia were married in 1920; Rikia was sixteen. In 1921 their son Najeeb was born in Regina, Saskatchewan.

Mahmoud purchased land in southern Alberta and moved his wife and son from the wide-open spaces of Saskatchewan to Alberta. Rikia, unaccustomed to rural life, adjusted in true pioneer spirit to country living. She and her mother would prepare three hot meals a day for eight to ten harvesters who worked from first light to sunset, depending on the weather. Twice a day Rikia would drive the 1929 model T Ford to the fields with the sandwiches and cold drinks for father and the crew until the harvesting was over. And then it was time to bring in the garden — vegetables and berries — and start weeks of canning in preparation for the cold, cold winter.

Six of Mahmoud and Rikia's children were born at home, attended by Amina and a local legend, country physician Doc Anderson. One daughter, Budr, was born in hospital in Bassano, Alberta. It was December and the snowdrifts had made the roads impassable for cars so mother was wrapped in quilts with hot bricks in a horse-drawn sleigh. With her husband and Doc Anderson, they set off for Bassano, an all-day journey.

As the first-generation children of immigrant parents we were given Arabic names with Anglicized versions. Najeeb became Jim, I became Ilene, Zainab became Jean, Budr became Betty, Amina became Alma, Khalid became Bob, Haidar became Edward, and Naef became Tom. We were taught about Islam by our parents and grandmother. I remember listening to my father read from the Qur'an. He had a beautiful voice, and often when we would be rushing through the house bent on whatever pursuit engaged us at the time, he would say in Arabic, "Stop what you are doing and listen!"

When we were old enough, we fasted throughout the month of Ramadan. We learned to appreciate that the pangs of hunger would only last between sunrise and sunset for a month. There were poor families near our farm who felt real hunger, and in difficult times, father would ask Hugh Herd, the owner of the country store, to send provisions but not to say who had sent them.

Our ranch was a prosperous mixed operation of cattle, horses, and grain. It was a happy time — "This is God's country," my father would say of the grazing pastures and fields of grain stretching to the horizon. Times would change and lack

Rikia Haidar Saddy (seated far right) and husband Mahmoud
(seated far left) and their children, 1949.

of rain changed the fertile landscape to what was to become
"next year's country." When the land could no longer support
the cattle, horses, and wheat fields, it was time to leave the land
and to move north to Cold Lake, Alberta to a rented farm, and
two years later in 1936, to Edmonton which became our second home. My father was semi-retired, but the land was so
much a part of him that he returned each summer to farm his
land in southern Alberta, where we joined him on school hol-
idays. While father was at the farm, mother was busy acquiring
a plot of land to build a family home where the children could
grow up in a safe environment. Our home was open to friends
and many visitors from all parts of the world. One of these visitors eventually became the Prime Minister of Pakistan and my
husband.

One of the earliest recollections of my childhood was a
statement by mother to father, "I am getting old." The day was
December 24th, mother's 25th birthday. I was only six years old,
but I remember being very sad that mother was old. It seems to
me now that many lifetimes have gone by since that day.

Father, mother, four sons and four daughters, and grand-mother Amina — we were a substantial addition to the small Muslim community in Edmonton. The families met in each other's homes to discuss the future of the community. They felt a mosque was needed where Muslim families in Edmonton and from surrounding areas could meet, offer prayers and socialize. In the 1930s, money was scarce, but with the help of fellow Muslims throughout the western provinces and the northern communities, Christian friends of Middle East origin, and from the larger community, a start was made. Mother and grand-mother, along with other women in the community, organized fundraising dinners and teas in their homes.

At last the dream was realized and the Al Rashid Mosque was completed in 1938 — the first mosque in North America. The mosque became the heart of the community, faithful to the Islamic concept of a meeting place, a place for prayers, Islamic studies, and when possible, the study of Arabic. Non-Muslims were welcome to visit and join in social events. In the basement kitchen of the mosque, the women produced wonderful food, supplemented by dishes from their own kitchens. As a family we attended prayers at the mosque, and there were close associa-tions with members of the community — a favorite time was open house after Eid prayers when many friends would visit and partake of special Eid foods.

The immigrants at that time were mainly from Syria, which was under French mandate until 1943. When France withdrew, Lebanon was born. From the time we were old enough, we were defending our origins and our faith based on facts not generally known — the Muslim and Arab contributions to mathematics, medicine, philosophy, and the Arabic numerals that replaced Roman numerals. It was often frustrating because the only exposure Westerners had was through Hollywood movies where Muslims and Arabs were depicted as villains. When registering for school in the 1940's, my youngest brother was asked, "What is your religion?" He replied that he was a Muslim. The teacher wrote down "heathen." Mother was upset by the West's misunderstanding of Islam but was angered even more by countries acting in un-islamic ways in the name of Islam.

Unlike today, the issue of covering our heads did not arise. On my first visit to Lebanon in the 1950s, all the Muslim girls in our mixed-faith village of Jib Jenine wore a head covering – a scarf of any size or color — tied at the nape of the neck. A few years later on another visit, the young women had abandoned the scarf and only the much older generation wore it. In my family we covered our heads only in the mosque or at prayers. We were to dress modestly and make-up was permitted only if applied in such an understated way that it looked natural.

My father died of cancer in 1951 at the age of 67. Mother was grief stricken by this loss. He had been her companion throughout most of her life in Canada. They were partners in all their endeavors, remaining strong in their faith and belief in family. Mother carried on with courage, keeping her family close to home. We were encouraged to bring our friends home both for studies and to plan school activities such as high-school elections. Mother continued her involvement in activities for the Al Rashid Mosque, and with other women organized the very successful annual mosque dinners to raise funds and to introduce non-Muslims to our food, culture, and place of worship.

In 1960 my brother Haidar and a friend travelled for over a year to more than 30 cities and four continents. In New Delhi, India, they stayed at a YMCA. In the lobby was a poster announcing that a man would speak that night about his recent trip to Canada. "As we were strong Canadian nationalists and somewhat homesick, we decided to attend the presentation to learn how others view our wonderful country," he recalls. "We were seated comfortably with approximately 30 others that evening and were enjoying the narrative and 8MM films of the speaker's journey across Canada. There was, of course, a swell of pride in the wonderful scenery and the flattering remarks of the speaker for the hospitality extended to him. As his travels took him to Edmonton, the scenes became more familiar. I sat up in my chair so as not to miss any familiar landmarks of our city and to hear his comments. His film showed the beautiful university campus, the High Level Bridge, which at 160 feet above the river, was the highest in Canada, and then a roadway that passes our home. To my amazement, the next sight was the exterior of my mother's home. The next scene was inside the home, where my mother was entertaining a group, including the

Rikia Haidar-Saddy (right)
and her daughter Aliya Mohammed Ali, 1974.

speaker who appeared to be a guest of honor at this dinner party. I was dumfounded that half-way around the world in a city I had never visited I would hear a stranger from Madras — also just visiting New Delhi — praise my mother's hospitality. I am certain there are many other films and photographs of my mother entertaining visitors to be found throughout Asia, Europe, and the Middle East. My hope is one day to be pleasantly surprised again when travelling in those areas."

Grandmother and mother had many sayings in Arabic which we learned over the years. One of mother's favorites: "Beauty will ultimately fade away but intellect and honor will forever endure." As time moves on we often remind each other of her words. Grandmother Amina was an important part of our lives. She spoke to us always in Arabic, and from childhood we learned about the exploits of legendary heroes — Haroun al Rashid Aantaar and many others — stories from Islamic history about the Prophet and his companions. The tales of life in the Bekaa Valley gave us a strong link with the land of our ancestors. The loss of our grandmother in 1955 at the age of 80 left a great void. For mother it was very difficult. They were devoted to each other, sharing their deep faith in their journey through life, supporting each other in the adjustments to new and strange countries with courage and patience. She died heart-broken over Zainab, the tragedy of her life. For days before her death she kept asking if it was Friday, and on Friday she passed away from us.

Our beautiful and gracious mother continued to be the pillar of her family. She was mother and friend, supporting each of us, listening to our problems, advising us and giving us her blessings. One by one we left home to pursue careers and marry. Now, we thought, mother would come and live with us in turn. But it was not to be — she loved us but valued her independence and declined to live with any of her children. She maintained her own home, always open to her many friends and family, drove herself to visit family and friends, and was happiest when she had her children and twenty grandchildren around her. She was thrilled with the arrival of her great-grandchildren. Over the years, her grandchildren loved to visit her to confide in her their plans or their problems — or to just ask her for one of her recipes. She was open to changes that took place around her and accepted the differences between the generations while remaining true to her values. She cooked delicious meals for us and sent "Zowadies" — food packages — home with us when we left.

Always ready for a new adventure, mother opened a ladies' fashion shop on Whyte Avenue and 104 Street and operated it with my sister Amina from 1953 to 1960. In addition to the Women's Muslim Association, she belonged to many other women's organizations and subscribed to the Symphony Society and the Citadel Theatre. Mother's love of travel took her to Lebanon and to Syria to visit family and on one occasion to settle family property to ensure that we would have our inheritance whenever we returned. She went to Egypt and Kuwait, Pakistan, Japan, and the Philippines. She loved life and was ready to travel to visit family, friends, or to see new countries and make new friends.

In the spring of 1977 mother returned to Mexico with my sister Zainab and her daughter Marilyn. Zainab describes the trip in her own words: "Mother was seventy-two years old and very healthy and active. She was happy and excited about the time we would spend in Mexico City. On our arrival we were greeted by Jorje — a young Mexican known to us through my brother Bob. On the way to our hotel, we asked Jorje if we could pass by the city square. He was confused as he could not place the square described by mother in the city centre or anywhere in the city. He said he would get a map and try to find it. It had been more than 60 years since mother had left Mexico, but she had retained the memory of a beautiful park where parents came and visited with each other while their children played in safety. That special park with beautiful flowers and vendors with snacks and sweets was engraved in her memory. We never found the park — it no longer existed.

"On the last day in Mexico City we visited the Pyramids. Mother insisted on climbing the tallest one — the Pyramid of the Sun. She climbed much higher than I did and the people watching were amazed and congratulated her — she was pleased and we were proud! We flew to Ixtapa the next day with a plan to rent a car and drive to Zhuatanayo. Mother seemed very distressed by this. She told us there were banditos — bandits — roaming the nearby hills and they would rob and kill us as we were defenceless women. She was recalling the warnings she had heard during the civil war when the rebels and bandits made it dangerous for anyone to travel. We had befriended a lady in our hotel and left mother with her before we drove off — reluctantly. We returned earlier than planned to find mother happy to see us and ready to join us in whatever adventure we planned for the next day. She seemed to have made peace with the fact that this was no longer the Mexico she had left more than half a century ago."

By 1988 the historic Al Rashid Mosque in Edmonton had to be moved to another location because the land on which it stood had been acquired by the Royal Alexandra Hospital. After many efforts to relocate the Al Rashid failed, the demolition was scheduled to go into effect after the fiftieth anniversary of the mosque. It was the granddaughters of the women who had so energetically made the Al Rashid possible that came to the rescue with the aid of a new breed of Muslim women from places like Northern Africa, Eastern Africa, the

Middle East, and the Indian Subcontinent. As one of the founding members of the Al Rashid, Rikia was very supportive of the ongoing efforts to save the mosque, as were all her children. Her granddaughter, my daughter, Mahmuda Ali, was one of those in the forefront of the five-year struggle along with Karen Hamdon, another granddaughter of a founding member. For these women, it was unacceptable to celebrate a fifty-year anniversary and then to have the mosque demolished. They spearheaded the Friends of the Al Rashid Mosque to obtain recognition of Al Rashid's historical value and the significance of Muslim contributions to Alberta. Despite tremendous opposition, the mosque was relocated to the Fort Edmonton Heritage Park. Today, the Al Rashid Mosque stands as a symbol of the reality of Islam in Canada. I am very proud of my daughter and all the other women for saving the mosque and having it placed in a heritage park where so many visitors will see it and learn about Islam.

On Friday, June 1, 1990, our beloved mother died at the age of 85. Before her peaceful death, she seemed to know that she would be leaving us and repeated her wish to each of us that we would take care of each other and remain close as a family. This we have endeavored to do to honor her wishes and her memory.

We learned so much about our family, faith, and culture from grandmother, Amina, and our parents. But there were many questions we should have asked, as there are gaps in our knowledge, and our children now want to know the answers. Often I have thought — as in the past — I'll ask mother. But mother isn't there anymore.

Aliya Mohammed Ali

Najabey

My name is Maryam Campbell and this is my mother's story. Her name was Najabey Jazey (her maiden name was Yassin) and she was born in 1905 in Karoun, Syria. My mother was eighteen when she married my father; it was an arranged marriage. He left for Canada in 1926 to join his father, mother, sister, and two brothers. Immigration officials changed my father and grandfather's surnames from Hejazey to Jazey as they said this would be easier to pronounce. My mother followed three years later with their two daughters aged five and four, Betty and Fatima. They boarded a ship to Halifax from Marseilles, France.

When my mother and sisters arrived in Halifax, they went through customs and boarded a train for Saskatchewan. Later on that train they were given food, including a stick of bologna. As Muslims, we don't eat pork. My mother did not know what kind of meat was in the bologna, so she put it on her seat until the train took off and then gave it to some of the other immigrants. My mother had sewn money into the pocket lining of her coat, and at one point she gave five-year-old Fatima some money so that the next time the train stopped she could get some fruit. When my sister came back, she had lots of fruit and lots of money. My mother was shocked at all the change she brought back. She knew nothing about our monetary system.

When my mother arrived in Shaunavon, Saskatchewan, she

was met by my father and other family members. During their first Christmas in Canada, Christian friends and neighbors realized my parents didn't have a tree so they chopped one down, decorated it, and brought it to their home. It was not Muslim tradition to have a tree, but over the years we continued to have a tree at that time of the year. We celebrated with family and good friends.

My sisters started school and began to learn the English language. The following year my eldest brother was born. With three children and a lot of chores, my mother was very busy. She would slaughter chickens, but she always said a prayer first for the animal so that it wouldn't suffer and to thank God for the food. My mother made our pillows, our quilts, and lambs' wool duvets. She also washed all the clothes by hand. My mother was never one to complain about all the hard work.

About 1932, my father's youngest brother died. They say it was tuberculosis. My mother was expecting her fourth child, and when she was born, she had three or four teeth. Her name was Laila. In those days the doctors felt the teeth had to come out. When they took the teeth out, the gums became infected, and the little girl died after fifteen days. Soon after, my father's mother, Maryam, who had also joined her family in Canada, became ill with stomach cancer. My mother had to look after my grandmother and administer the medicine and the morphine. After three deaths, my parents looked forward to my arrival in 1934. I was born in a hospital, the only one out of seven children.

There was massive drought and unemployment and my father's shoemaking business and pool hall weren't doing well. Soon my parents couldn't manage any longer, and on the advice of my grandfather, who had already moved to Nova Scotia, they decided to follow him. My grandfather had told them it was much nicer in Nova Scotia, that everything grows beautifully. There were also more Muslim families there.

My father had an old Ford. He had a trailer built and attached it to the back of the car. So my mother, my father, my aunt Aisha, uncle Joe, and my two sisters, Betty and Fatima, my brother Moe, and I all piled in. It was 1935 and many of

Najabey Jazey (center) with close relatives, 1981

the roads weren't paved. It was summer and the heat was unbearable. With four children in tow and another one on the way, it was a tough trip for my mother. She told me that although it was tiring, she enjoyed seeing the country and having many picnics.

My own memories of my mother actually begin in Nova Scotia. We lived in Day Spring, which was just a few miles out of Bridgewater. To make ends meet, my mother picked berries and dandelion greens and sold them for a dime. My sisters used to pick alongside her while I sat with my brother on a blanket and had to be very quiet. That money sustained us for the winter. One winter my mother had over a hundred dollars saved from berries and greens. We had neighbors who would make butter and my mom used to barter back and forth. I remember her buying great big galvanized tanks of milk to make yoghurt and cheese.

My mother would also take sheepskin and treat it with a coarse salt and nail it to the side of a barn to dry. She would clean, dry, and separate the wool. I can remember my feet touching those beautiful wool rugs on cold, cold mornings. This was before wall-to-wall carpeting. I remember the long lines of sheets and clothes she washed. On a summer day she would make soap outside. I remember that one of the ingredients was lye, and she would take this big pot and have a great big paddle in it. It looked like a witch's brew. She would make this to last for a year. She would sew beautiful tunics using my father's trousers as material and she would make them look like new. The sugar bags and the flour bags were all kept and bleached and she would embroider on them so they looked like flowers in a field.

A day started very early in the morning and ended sometimes at midnight and even later, according to what she had to do. There was a lot of sewing with an old Singer pedal machine that she used. It wasn't just the clothes. She made coats and quilts. I have two quilts left that she made with my grandmother. They must have taken an awful long time, but I think that she saw the result of her work. She also crocheted. It took her two years to crochet a beautiful tablecloth for me that I still have and hold dear to my heart. I can't do a lot of things that she could do, I'm envious really, but I must admit, though, that I picked up the cooking from her quite well. I'm noted for my cooking. My mother would make her own bread. Now this is the old way of doing it in the old country. You know these pizza parlors where they toss the dough up in the air and fling it around, well, my mother's method was similar to that, but not as flamboyant. I think it is an art form and I don't think there are too many people in this day and age who can do it.

Local people used to come to see my mother's garden because she was one of the first to grow green peppers and eggplants. She grew enough food in those gardens to last for the whole winter. She grew beans, tomatoes, potatoes, vegetable marrow — the list goes on. Her coosa and grape leaves were preserved in brine. We didn't have a freezer, so pickles were made, jams were made, all by a woman who couldn't read Arabic or English. Luckily we lived right at the mouth of the Atlantic and got fresh fish every day. I remember a fisherman giving my father pounds and pounds of lobster. I never liked it, even so, today the price is out of reach. People were very good at helping one another. This is the way it was.

I attended school in a two-room schoolhouse, Day Spring. As one of the younger children I was put at the very back of the class, so I actually didn't learn anything. Around Christmas, we were told Santa Claus was coming to the school concert. I desperately wanted to go. My youngest brother, Khalid, was not well so my mother didn't want to leave him or have a neighbour look after him. Recognizing my strong need to see Santa Claus, my mother bundled up my sick brother and myself, put us in a wagon, and pulled us through the deep snow for about a mile-and-a-half to school! She had even brought Arabic bread with cheese or peanut butter in case we got hungry on the way. I'll never forget her trudging through the deep snow as long as I live. At the time I didn't appreciate it, now I look back and wonder how she did it.

My mother was very religious. She fasted every year and prayed five times a day and taught me my prayers. Years later when I asked to go to church with my Christian Arab friends, my mother allowed me to go. She said, "You can go to that church, and you can pray, you must remember that all churches are the house of God, but you pray in our way to God. He's the same God." She also said that my faith was part of my soul, it couldn't be taken away, that I was born Muslim and would die Muslim.

We moved to Kentville in 1940 or 1941. My father opened a shoemaker's shop for people with foot problems and he would make shoes from scratch. A few years later my father took on a restaurant. It was an enterprise that hadn't gone well for other people, but succeeded with us. My mother, father, sisters and my brother Moe, we all had to work in this restaurant. My parents hired a couple of waitresses and dishwashers. I remember my mom getting up at four or five in the morning and getting the stove and the furnace going, and then leaving for the restaurant to heat up the big stoves and ovens for the day. Her speciality was pies and she had the recipes in her head. She would make twenty to thirty pies for the day during the Apple Blossom Festival, and then come home to more work.

As a little girl during the war, I wanted to help the war effort so I put on a play and a movie in our garage. One of the neighbor boys had his father's projector to show a cartoon and I put on a play. We charged ten cents admission. My mother made donuts and lemonade that we sold for five cents. We made $16.11 and sent it to the Red Cross. In return we got a beautiful letter of thanks.

In 1941 the last child was born, Moody. That night the men were all downstairs and my mother was upstairs and the doctor was attending to her. My mother's friend, Mrs Joseph, was sharing my bed with me. We heard this wailing, and when the child was born, Mrs Joseph jumped out of bed to help the doctor and my mother. Mrs Joseph was one of the many Arabs who felt a kinship toward us and helped us. Even though she didn't have time for herself, my mother told me she was so happy with these women who shared her language and customs. Many were Christian Arabs from a village not far from where my mother and father came from. I called them aunt and uncle and we went to their celebrations and they came to ours.

We used to have people stay in our home overnight as they travelled through town. I remember we had a young Jewish couple come and visit us. They were from Cuba. My sister Betty brought them to the house to meet the family. They mentioned something about eating pork, and my mother jumped out of her seat. She said, "You don't eat pork in your religion! You don't eat it! We don't eat it! You're not supposed to eat it!" They were taken aback. I think it kind of scared them a little bit. But mother was just trying to remind them of who they were.

Around Easter my mother would take me to the local store to get a new coat, a new hat, a pair of shoes, and a new dress, and even gloves. We used to have a music festival every year and that dress was for the occasion. Unfortunately, my mother didn't get out to many of our school activities in those days. I remember winning a prize in school and looking in the audience to see if my mother was there. She wasn't. It was the first and only time that I ever won anything in school.

My mother was strict with her children. No make-up, no shorts, no lingering in bathing suits after a swim, no dancing, and definitely no boyfriends. As her daughters got older, my

Najabey Jazey (seated) and her daughters, 1981

mother felt we should try to mingle with more Muslims as her dream was for us to marry into our own faith. There was a Muslim family in Bridgetown and my mother wanted to move there. My father purchased a general store there. It had a section for groceries and a section for men's wear. When we moved, my mother had a lot of responsibility, cleaning and filling the shelves. She couldn't read, so you can imagine what it was like to make out the labels, but she did it all and did it well.

A great change began to take place in my father's life, probably because of stress and the uncertainty of his business. He became belligerent and difficult and began to drink; the alcohol made him very ill tempered. My mother sometimes threatened to leave. In 1953 she finally did. I came home to find my father alone and sobbing. He had been drinking, and I told him I was glad mom had left. I yelled at him about how he had never treated her well and that if he wanted her back, he would have to stop drinking.

Najabey Jazey (seated, front center), and her husband
Mohammed Jazey (seated, front), and their children.
Maryam Campbell is standing in the back row, 1981.

He promised to stop and my mom came back. But it would take another ten years before he gave up alcohol for good. Even though this tension was all around us, my mother never talked to her children about the drinking, but she did confide in close friends. In the mid-'50s business was slowing down because the larger grocery franchises moved into town. My father was not spending time in the business, so the responsibility of the business fell to my mother and my brother Moe. A lot of people didn't realize what she was going through. She always remained at my father's side and helped him in any way that she could. This was her job; this is how she felt, and despite those difficult times she kept the family together. In 1968 my father retired. After that, he and my mother went everywhere together.

In the early 1960s, my mother and I became involved in an adult education religion class. People of different faiths attended this class. My mother took this very seriously and enjoyed it so much. My youngest brother, Moody, was in the air force so my mother became a member of the legion as well.

As a young woman I left home and fell in love with a man who was not Muslim. My mom was terribly disappointed. She sent me to live with my aunt Dorothy in Windsor for a year to see if I would meet a Muslim man. If after the year I still wanted to marry the non-Muslim, she would agree to the wedding. This is exactly what happened. I became more devout over the years because I was married to a non-Muslim and I wanted to hold on to my faith. We never fought about religion, and he never converted. Although she wasn't educated in the way we think of education today, my mother was far ahead in her thinking. She used to say to me that I should never force my husband to convert. Touching her heart, she said, "It must come from here." My three brothers also married out of the faith and have had successful marriages. My two sisters never married and stayed with my parents until they died. So my three children became their children. My children will tell you that they had many mothers. Betty joined the Red Cross and worked as a Red Cross aid. She worked in one of the homes for people who had psychological problems. She taught one boy to read. She used to go up nearly every night so he could at least learn to write his name. Those were painstaking hours. She taught English to immigrants, in particular, a family from Lebanon. She also taught Arabic cooking in adult education classes. Fatima started the Kentville drama group and directed virtually every single Noel Coward play. She was also a talented director and wrote poems and song lyrics. All these accomplishments are put away in a box somewhere, in a storage room.

When I had my own three children, my mother adored them. She wanted them with her constantly and she got upset if I said that I was going curling and I was getting a baby-sitter. She had so much time for them as she was not working very much. She also spent her time taking day trips to nearby places and watching television.

Early in her life in Canada my mother spoke of regrets she had over leaving the Arab world. Life wasn't that easy in the old country, but I think she had fared a little better than she did when she came over to Canada. In those early days my mother did a lot of things that most pioneer women in that day and age had to do. She probably wasn't that different from any other immigrant woman, even in her regrets over leaving Syria. But after a visit to her village in 1971, she said she would never go back to Syria. She had found generous and kind people in Nova Scotia, loved the marvellous summers and the freedom to do what she wanted. Canada had really become home to her.

From 1974 to 1980, there was always a death in the family. My mother would be the first one to go down to the home and organize the dinner. We call it the mercy dinner. We served a mercy dinner for every member of our family that died. People never really started the dinners until she got there.

Then on January 15th, 1982 my mother died of pancreatic cancer in Bridgetown. In her final days she wanted to come home from the hospital as she knew she was dying. Her children and her husband surrounded her. We read the Qur'an to her and prayed with her. She was buried in the local cemetery so my father and the rest of the family could go and visit the grave. Despite their difficulties, their last fifteen years together had been happy ones, and there is no doubt in my mind they loved each other. Hundreds came to my mother's funeral. The Archdeacon of the Anglican Church, C.R. Elliott, sent a letter to my family, thanking my mother for showing him our ways. He respected her for the way she had conducted herself as a Muslim.

My father died at the age of 96 in 1998. He had outlived two of his daughters; Fatima died in 1988 of liver cancer and Betty died of lung cancer in 1992. There are four of us left now — myself, Moe, Khalid, and Moody.

I often remember that when things didn't go right and I got depressed, my mother would tell me, "There's always a little sadness, but it's always followed by something good, so it will come. Maybe not tomorrow, but it will come." With all the difficult times she had, she seemed to carry through. I kind of like to think that this is what life is all about. In spite of the difficult times, our home was a good home and we knew we were loved. There are things that are hard for me to explain, things that my mother taught me, the sincerity in her voice, the convictions she had. You know, treating people with fairness. I only think of those good things now.

Maryam Campbell

This story is dedicated to my brothers
Moe, Khalid, and Moody Jazey.

Lila

My life is a journey, a spiritual journey that began almost seven and a half decades ago. As I think back to how it all began, I realize how fortunate I have been. My mother was American-born. Her parents, staunch Methodists of English ancestry, farmed in Nebraska. Mother's family tree goes all the way back to Zachary Taylor, an American general, who was called "Rough and Ready," and who became the twelfth President of the United States. Zachary Taylor didn't believe in racism, and many people think this brought about his sudden death. Mother always said he had been poisoned.

My father was a pillar of the Muslim community in rural southern Saskatchewan. His lineage can be traced back to the Prophet Muhammad and more recently to the 12th century Sufi saint Abd al Qadir from Jillani, Iraq. He was born in Lala, in the Bekaa Valley in Lebanon. He did not believe in fighting and left Lebanon in 1900 to escape conscription by the Turkish army. He came to North America by boat with a friend, and while his friend was allowed to get off in Halifax, my father had to stay on the boat until he reached New York. To make a living, he bought all kinds of household goods wholesale and then sold them door to door.

My parents met in the spring of 1910 in Nebraska. My father was travelling across the United States by horse and buggy peddling his household goods. On a country road in Nebraska he saw a tall, fair-haired girl working in a farmyard.

As he climbed down from his buggy, the girl vanished. For my father it was love at first sight. He pursued young Chelsea Pritchard and within a few weeks 16-year-old Chelsea and 43-year-old Sied planned to elope because Chelsea's parents objected to their daughter marrying a Muslim. They travelled to North Dakota where a relative of my father was getting married. That wedding became a double wedding. From North Dakota my parents went to Brandon, where my father's friend Ahmed Awid had opened a wholesale business. He told my mother that his home was her home.

After a few months the newlyweds travelled to Sheho, Saskatchewan. The only way to build a house on the sparse prairie was to dig sod in the shape of a brick. My mother cleared the land of stones with a horse pulling a stone boat. Water was carried from a nearby creek. Soon their first son, Saleem, was born with the help of a neighbor who was a midwife.

Life was difficult, and my father became anxious to travel, so they packed their belongings into a buckboard and moved to Regina. Here my father helped build the first railway connecting the city from east to west. My father got itchy feet again and he moved his family to Swift Current where he had heard there was a Lebanese family. He bought a homestead for five dollars in Hamilton Grove, just south of the town. That August my brother, Ameen, was born. My father built a log cabin with poplar trees.

The land was flat virgin prairie and this was a blessing in disguise. My family lived in fear of fire and watched the flat horizon for any sign of smoke. When there was a fire, people loaded their buggies with water, sacks, and pitchforks. One day there was smoke at our friends, the Kaziels. When my father arrived, he climbed a haystack, faced east and called "God is great" several times in Arabic. The wind was blowing so hard it almost swallowed his words. Suddenly, the wind stopped and the fire burned into itself. Muslim families in Western Canada still tell this story.

In 1912 we had a fire on our own farm, and according to my mother, my father prayed until the fire went out. In the old country, my grandmother, a Sufi, would ride a horse over people lying on the road. This was a test of faith; those who

Lila Fahlman, 1974.

had faith would not feel the hooves. My grandmother's name was Lila; I was named after her. She came from a family renowned for its healers; I've been told my great-great-grandfather could walk across a bed of hot coals without burning his feet!

Often local bachelors would come to our farm to have one of my mother's dinners. One day a neighbor came over, tied his horse to the fence, took a paper bag from his buggy, and hid it behind a huge rock pile. After dinner he went out to retrieve the bag. He ran back into the house, glaring at my mother. "How did you know?" he demanded. My mother told him she couldn't be fooled where alcohol was involved. She had emptied the liquor from the bottles and smashed them. No one drank in her house!

Lila Fahlman and her father, 1927.

I was born in 1924 and my earliest recollections are of a red Hudson's Bay blanket. This blanket was my world, where I lay on my tummy and wiggled or fell asleep. When I was four years old, my parents took me to Moose Jaw to have my picture taken. I wore a beautiful soft green dress with a matching wide corded ribbon across my forehead and tied at the back into a bow. A beautiful strand of pearls from Uncle Albert completed the picture. It was one of two times that I wore new clothes. Then there was the Whippet car. I used to sit in the back seat with mother's plants and my 'dog', which was not real. I used to cut the dog's hair constantly for I imagined it to be growing. I was too young to realize that toy dogs do not have real hair.

It was at this time, at the age of five, that I began to learn about the power of prayer. I had listened to many stories told by others about my father and his ancestors and the gift of the sprit and the power of prayer. I remember one day in particular when I wanted to mend my plush toy dog. I needed thread and a needle. I searched and searched, but none was to be found. I took my little blue Qur'an and began to pray and I kept praying and praying for this needle and thread. I remember finding it and the joy that I felt when I was able to mend my toy dog.

Mother had inherited a small sum of money when her father passed away in Nebraska and soon we were on the road to Regina. Our new home became the rooms behind Dad's new People's store. I was fascinated by a slit in the door that was really a mail slot. I used to slip candy to my friends. My father reminded me that the store was a business, where my parents needed to make money, and that I was not to give away free candy. I often crawled through the opening between my bed and the store to reach the candy counter. We sold halvah, which was my favorite kind of candy. Later, father found a larger store with nicer living accommodations in the back. He sold the first store.

Tom Mortensen from Holland lived in our basement. He used to teach me songs in Dutch and German that I remember to this day. He used to spread lard on his bread. I would tease him about it. He would yell and throw his cup of tea after me as I ran up the stairs. I really liked him. He was like a grandfather to me. Years later, on Halloween night, I was told that old Tom had passed away. As I scrubbed the Halloween make-up off my face, I cried and cried into the basin of water. I had lost my "grampa."

My older brother, Saleem, became a policeman. There was not much crime then, just the mischief of a few teenagers. One day my younger brother, Ameen, took Saleem's buffalo coat which was part of the police uniform, he also wore his brother's police hat, and rode his bike up and down the street to scare the kids. The chief of police later summoned Saleem into his office and suggested he control his younger brother's shenanigans.

In the 1930s, the Depression hit Regina. Business after

business fell victim. People would come to beg for food with promises to pay later. My father had a big heart. The government came to the rescue of many people when it set up the process called 'relief'. Once a month, everyone got a small sum of money to buy food. Our customers began to go to Eaton's with their relief checks. They came to us for food on credit when their relief ran out. Before the end of the month they would beg at our door for food for which they would pay "later." After a few months of this, we found ourselves lined up for relief checks along with our customers. Our business died and our home was gone. All we had was the small relief check that barely fed us. We found a very small house that we rented from the relief agency.

It was at this time that I started school. I remember mother packing a lunch for me. I ate it outside against the school wall, but I was so homesick that within minutes I ran home, much to my mother's surprise. She took me by my hand and walked me back to school, scolding me all the way. When winter came, it was a long, cold walk to school. I wore a toque on my head and someone's old suit jacket fastened together at the neck with a huge safety pin, long underwear, brown ribbed stockings, and galoshes over my shoes.

Wetmore Elementary School was a large brick building with the words "Boys" and "Girls" imprinted above each door. A cement walkway led from the road to the school. We were told in no uncertain terms that neither boys or girls crossed over the walkway. But many a time, the boys came very close to the line to get a good look at the girls, who were also close to their side of the line.

One day I made the mistake of wearing the pearls Uncle Albert gave me to school. One of the girls reached over to touch my pearls. Another girl decided to do the same thing. Before I knew it, the cord snapped and my big beautiful pearls lay on the ground. Everyone began to pick up the pearls. I had only a few in my hand when I saw the girls running away with the rest.

We moved to Winnipeg Street. There were three huge garden lots north of our house that my father leased from the city. He always grew beautiful gardens, but this was the first time he had such a large area to plant. Little did I realize that I would become part of this operation. When I was not in school, I spent the summers carrying two grape baskets filled with produce from my father's garden. Every morning and afternoon, all summer long, I went from apartment to apartment, house to house, until all of the fresh vegetables were sold. I remember my father's promise that I would be rewarded with a bicycle. I never did get a bicycle; we needed the money from the vegetables for day to day necessities.

On the corner, north of us, there was a lumberyard. In front of the lumberyard, where Victoria Avenue and Winnipeg Street meet, there was a huge mansion. I met Nellie, who lived in the big mansion. We became close friends. She often took me through the different rooms of the house. It was three stories tall and had a 'secret' stairway from the kitchen to the third floor. This stairway was used by the servants. Many a warm night Nellie and I would sleep in our makeshift tent, made from old gunnysacks and huge nails.

Across the street from our house was the fire hall. We were very good friends with the firemen. Once a week my father would take vegetables from the garden and the firemen would put everything together in a huge pot and make 'mulligan' stew. Tommy Jackson was my favorite fireman. He cut my hair when it grew too long. He always had tears in his eyes when he cut my hair. Tommy did not have any children, so I was his little girl. Everyone admired my blond hair. My dad used to kiss it everyday.

In elementary school I skipped grade two. I also fought with Isabelle Mackay, a fireman's daughter, and broke her glasses. In grade five I had an assignment on line perspectives that I made into a booklet. On the last page I drew a scene of a living room using all the various perspectives. I got the highest mark in the class. Isabelle had difficulty completing her assignment so Miss King gave her my copy to help her. Isabelle traced everything I had done, including my living room picture. She made a mess of my original work but got a perfect mark. I was so hurt. I could not believe that the teacher would give perfect marks to her for copying my work.

My friend Isabelle was a redhead. She and I loved to skate.

We would put our skates and socks in the warm oven of the wood-stove before putting them on our feet. Then we would walk five blocks to the open-air rink to enjoy our skating. I used to rub my bare feet with menthol to keep them warm. Many were the times that I would go skating alone late at night, I loved it so much.

A highlight for me in school was the music class. Miss Merle Andrews took our chorus into the Spring Music Festival, and every year we won first prize. I took private singing lessons from her for twenty-five cents a lesson. She looked like Wallis Warfield Simpson, the Prince of Wales' lady friend. When the radio announced that the Prince of Wales was to become our King Edward VIII, the newspapers began carrying the story that he wanted to marry Simpson, a divorcée. All hell broke loose in London, England. I could not see why he should not marry the woman of his choice, but the powers that be said there should be no divorcée in the Royal Family. So King Edward abdicated the throne of England rather than lose the woman he loved.

For many years to come my garments came from a church in the neighborhood, St. Matthew's Anglican Church. When I reached my teens, I met Mary who was older than I and had beautiful clothes that she gave to me. I wanted so much to give something to her. One night, mother and I were at a function where they drew prizes. I won a beautiful silver chaffing dish. This I gave to Mary. She sat on the carpet holding the chaffing dish. She turned it slowly in her hands, exclaiming her joy at receiving such a beautiful gift. She was my very best friend. Years later Mary got married and we drifted apart, but I always remember her with much joy.

My mother was a very politically minded person. She took me everywhere she went. In those days, you never had a babysitter. When my parents visited friends, the evening ended with me falling asleep, with my head on someone's kitchen table. My father would carry me on his back, all the way home.

The summer of 1935 began as a quiet one. Men were out of work, and every conversation centered on this fact. People still came and knocked on doors for food. Psychologically, it was very demeaning. There was much unrest in the West. In Vancouver, men began gathering and organizing into groups. They wanted to go to Ottawa to state their case before Members of Parliament. They had no money and no means of transportation, so they decided to 'ride the rods'. It was illegal. If the Mounties caught them, they risked being shot or arrested, but there was no other way to get to Ottawa. Hundreds of these men arrived in Regina. They were 'housed' in the exhibition grounds. A meeting was planned for Saturday night at the Market Square in downtown Regina. Hundreds of people came, including women and children. The men climbed up to the platform. They spoke about their own personal problems. Some were more political than others.

All of a sudden, there was a loud bang. There were large moving vans parked to the north of the Market Square. The bang was the huge doors opening. Suddenly, RCMP on horseback rode out of the vans and into the crowds of people. Women screamed and children cried. My mother grabbed my hand and we started to run away from the square. Some people were killed, many others were hurt. We were fortunate that we were not in the center of the market. In fact, we were at the opposite end of the square from the moving vans. Word was that Ottawa ordered the so-called 'March to Ottawa' to be stopped in Regina. There were rumors that men were arrested for hanging around the train stations waiting to grab a freight train to Ottawa.

In Regina, three boys from the East End were found dead on the train tracks. They had been run over by a freight train. Their heads were severed from their bodies. The Mounties reported that they had been sleeping on the track. Everyone knew that the boys would have heard the trains from a great distance. Besides why would they use the train track as a pillow? In those days, coffins had a glass window, and during the funeral I saw the three boys with their heads sewn back on. That scene is as vivid in my mind today as it was more than sixty years ago.

In 1936 we moved to a cottage home on Atkinson Street, a few blocks north of the power plant. Not far from the plant was a swimming hole where my friends and I swam. It was a very dangerous place, but we did not have any other place to go until the City of Regina dug a lake near the legislature to create jobs. The unemployed, many on relief, created islands in the lake and people could rent boats and go to the islands.

The girl next door, Helen Hoyer, had built a cardboard clubhouse in her backyard. I enjoyed listening to music there. The music came from cylinders, not flat records. We did not have a radio. In those days you had to pay for a license to have a radio. People who had radios were afraid to play them for fear they'd be found out and lose their radios. We listened to KOA Denver and KSL Salt Lake City.

I never missed a day of school until I got chicken pox. The truant officer showed up at my house because he did not want me to start playing hooky as one of my brothers had. When I finished grade eight, I had little intention of going on to high school. The tuition fee was eleven dollars a year, but for a family on relief it may as well have been a thousand dollars. When the principal, Mr Detwiler, asked me why I wasn't going on to high school, I told him we could not afford it. He was persistent and told me not to worry about the fee. In high school I didn't think much about how that fee got paid, but it must have been the principal. I wish I had known what really happened so I could have thanked him and in later years paid back my debt.

In 1939 Queen Elizabeth and King George IV toured Canada. As a Girl Guide I was one of six chosen to be the Guard of Honour for the royal couple's Regina visit. I saluted and shook hands with the royalty. Queen Elizabeth was so beautiful, her eyes were so blue, and her skin perfect. I had never seen anyone so lovely. King George had a beautiful tan complexion, but later we heard that he had not been well on the tour. When Princess Diana was killed in 1997 I wrote to the Queen Mother and the Queen, expressing my sorrow. I also told the Queen Mother about being part of her Guard of Honour in 1939. She replied, surprised that I would remember her beauty after all these years.

In high school I listened to a radio program called "Roving Cowboy" every morning at seven. The cowboy had a beautiful voice. The songs he sang were songs of that era preceding the war. One of my friends at school told me that the cowboy, Al Fahlman, was her boyfriend, and she wanted to bring him over

Lila and Al Fahlman in Edmonton, Alberta, 1945.

to my house. I told her not to bother, but she turned up with
him a few days later. He met my father and spent the entire
evening talking to my father about religion, much to the disgust
of his girlfriend. Al was raised as a Catholic. He was very close
to his father who had left the Catholic Church. The father had
told his son that he hoped he would one day find his own religion. Al's conversations with my father about a faith that said
Jesus was not God brought Al closer to a religion that shared

his father's values. When Al's father died, his mother did not have the five hundred dollars for the priest to get her husband into purgatory. Al decided to convert to Islam.

Al also joined the Royal Canadian Air Force. One day he wrote from Montreal, asking my father for my hand in marriage. My father said it was my decision; I was not interested in marriage. A few months later another letter, and the same reply from my father. When I graduated from grade 12, I changed my mind and travelled to Montreal to marry Al. I left home with a dollar in my pocket and a box of fruit to last me for the four-day train journey. When I got off the train in Montreal, I bought a pair of nylons for a quarter and had some tea and toast for a dime. I found St. Catherine Street and took a bus to the military training school. It took me half an hour to get on the streetcar, I was in tears. I had tried to board the car from the front, until a passer-by stopped to tell me to board the car from the rear. At the training school I was told that Al was on duty and had sent four of his friends to take care of me.

Later Al introduced me to a lovely Lebanese family that welcomed me into their home. I stayed with them until our wedding day. I worked at Steinberg's and later at The Chick-n-Coup, answering phones in the office. I will always remember Fleurette, the cashier, and Smitty, the chef. Smitty always spoiled me with great food and rich desserts. Needless to say, I put on weight. Every day I ran through the red-light district to get to work and home again. Even though no one bothered me, I was afraid. The odd cab driver would ask me if I wanted a ride home. I always said no and ran even faster.

One day Al and I were in downtown Montreal to get a ring and our marriage licence. All of a sudden Al decided he wanted to get married that day. I said no. I had already bought a wedding dress and had ordered a three-tier wedding cake. But as we passed a church Al went straight to the manse, found a minister, and asked him to marry us. The minister agreed, but we needed witnesses. Al ran into the street and by coincidence saw my landlord and a friend. So there I was in my pale blue scarf, sweater, and skirt getting married. A day later our friends threw a party with a cake, but they were disappointed that they had not been part of the marriage ceremony.

Lila Fahlman's first teaching assignment at Hope Hill School near Broadview, Saskatchewan, 1942.

Shortly after Al was sent to St. John, New Brunswick, and I followed him by train. There was a lady with the Traveller's Aid Society at the station to meet me. The next day I got a job at a Greek restaurant. That evening, Al walked in with his friends. I dropped a tray of dishes and got fired. Within days I left St. John and returned to Montreal to live with an Italian family. Dr Mancuso had been in a detention camp because he was Italian. In the camp, he had been stabbed in the face and sent home. His wife made a living by embroidering the air force 'wings'. She worked late into the night, sitting on a high stool, bent over a slanted table. I can still see her face by the light as she stitched and stitched. Her daughter Mary made Italian pasta and salad with vinegar for us everyday.

I decided I wanted to become a mental health nurse. When I went to Regina to see my bother Saleem, he told me there was a great demand for teachers. He convinced me to take a nine-week teaching course at a technical school. I enrolled, and at the end of three weeks, the principal rushed into the class and announced an

Lila Fahlman runs for political office, 1971,
the first Muslim woman in Canada to do so.

urgent need for teachers. He asked if anyone would be willing to start teaching immediately; three of us put up our hands. I was assigned to Hope Hill School near Broadview, Saskatchewan. One of my students was a boy who was a bit of an outcast. He used to stand outside the window at recess and smoke. When I ignored the smoking, he would ask me why I didn't give him the strap for smoking. I told him I didn't think he needed the strap. Over the one winter I taught at the school, he and I became great friends.

Al was moved from New Brunswick to Manitoba. When the Alaska Highway was built he was posted to many communities along the highway, but was based in Edmonton. I bought a dress designer business in Calgary and worked twelve-hour days, sewing by machine or hand, without patterns. I sewed the gowns for the governor's ball; I loved the creative work. One woman who was pregnant asked me to design an outfit she could wear on the golf course right until the baby was due! My clients were wealthy people who wanted good clothes and the business made a profit. Around the same time Al was transferred to Winnipeg and wanted me to go with him. I loved my work and sewed until three and four in the morning but I was exhausted. So I just let the business go and moved to Winnipeg. A few years later, Al and I started a family; we eventually had three children, two girls and a boy, so my days were very busy. Today all three children are teachers.

In the early 1970s I ran for political office. During the 1971 election I ran for the federal New Democratic Party, but didn't get the nomination. At the time I was the first Muslim woman in Canada to run for political office.

In 1979, I was asked by the Canadian Muslim Council of Canada to sit on their board as the representative of Muslim women in Canada. At that time, my brother was also on the board, so I accepted the position. A year later I decided that I would rather be at home. I was attending board meetings where I had no vote. Therefore, Muslim women had no vote. So I offered my resignation to the board. They refused to accept it. I told them that if I was to truly represent Muslim women in Canada, I had to get to know them. After further discussions with the board, I suggested I travel across Canada to meet Muslim women in every city. I spent two summers travelling from Newfoundland to British Columbia, meeting and talking with my Muslim sisters, and it became clear that the women needed to have their own organization. I promised them that when I was finished travelling, I would call them together somewhere in central Canada. I chose the mosque in Winnipeg for our gathering. The sisters who lived in Winnipeg provided accommodation. We drew up a constitution, elected our executive, collected fees, and filed the necessary documents for incorporation. We were on our way to becoming the Canadian Council of Muslim Women (CCMW), with chapters in every province. We planned our first conference for the fall of 1982. News of our decision was received positively but there were a couple of exceptions.

That year I also started the first Arabic language program at the Canadian Islamic Centre in Edmonton; I had never had the opportunity to learn Arabic, the language of the Qur'an, so I found a teacher so the children could have an opportunity to learn it. Soon I decided the Muslim children needed to mix with their peers in the public school system and that Arabic should be taught as a heritage language. I was a counsellor at a junior high school at the time and went to a school board meeting where I met a woman who wanted Chinese taught as a heritage language. We made a joint submission and the board eventually approved our requests. Today Arabic is taught as a heritage language in two grade schools, two junior high schools, and one senior high school.

One year I did doctoral research on Lebanese Muslim students in two high schools. In speaking with students and teachers I discovered racism was very much an issue. One teacher actually told me she couldn't stand Arabs, but when asked about a specific student, she told me she was very fond of this person. She was shocked when I told her that the student is an Arab. When I finished my research, I received my Doctorate in Educational Psychology. That year I was also elected to the Edmonton Public School Board, the first Muslim woman in Canada to sit on a school board.

Muslim women in Edmonton were also pioneers in other ways. They were instrumental in building the first mosque in North America. They collected funds from the Muslim communities in Western Canada and from Edmonton businesses along Jasper Avenue. People of many other faiths contributed to the building of the mosque.

In the late 1980s, the city of Edmonton wanted to demolish the Al Rashid Mosque. The mosque was very precious to me. It was there I prayed next to Hilwie Hamdon, a spirited woman who reminded me of my mother. My fighting spirit came from my mother. She never remained silent in the face of injustice. I always believed that my angels were with me, and my strong belief in my Creator reassured me. Every day I am reminded of how close and how caring my angels are to me. I learned this lesson very early in life. I came from a family with a very strong faith. I was fortunate to inherit that faith.

The fight to save the mosque brought back memories of a similar fight in 1965. Back then the University of Alberta and the government of Alberta joined forces to eliminate a few dozen homes for university expansion. Among them was Rutherford House, a historic home used by a fraternity. I had talked with several people, including Hazel McCuaig, daughter of Alexander Rutherford, and other local well-known people. We had held meetings, and formed an executive and became the Society for the Preservation of Historical Homes. For five years, we had tried to persuade the Social Credit Government of the day to save Rutherford House. In 1971 I had approached the opposition, Peter Lougheed and Lou Hyndman, with our problem. I turned over our large file of correspondence with the Social Credit Government, as well as local estimates on the restoration of Rutherford House. Peter Lougheed promised to save Rutherford House if his party got elected. He did get elected and Rutherford House was saved.

Armed with that experience from the '60s, I shared the history of Rutherford House with the national CCMW and the local chapter in Edmonton. We started to lobby the City of Edmonton. We met with two women from Parks and Recreation to discuss moving the mosque to Fort Edmonton. The locations they suggested were demeaning for a mosque. I closed my book and said, "Thank you, but it appears that we, as Muslims, are being discriminated against, since there are five other places of worship in Fort Edmonton. Our mosque, which is facing demolition by the city, is said not to suit the criteria to be in Fort Edmonton with the churches there." I informed them that I would call a press conference. Suddenly a map of Fort Edmonton was removed from a briefcase and spread out on the large oak table. "Where would you like the Mosque to go?" they asked.

We won.

The Mosque now stands on a hill in Fort Edmonton Park. In 1998, we began our final restoration, a library on the lower floor of the mosque.

Today I chair the World Interfaith Education Association, and I am vice-chair of the North American Interfaith Network and vice-chair of Vision TV, a national network dedicated to multifaith dialogue. In 1993, as a memorial to the women of Bosnia, I founded and incorporated the World Council of Muslim Women Foundation. In 1998 I travelled on behalf of the foundation to China to meet with a group of local Muslim

Lila Fahlman (front), and the women who helped relocate the Al Rashid Mosque, on the steps of the mosque in its new location, 1996.

Lila Fahlman with children in China, 1998.

women in Xinjinang Province. I wanted to know what they needed to educate their children. I was overwhelmed by their hospitality and the love and attention from the young people. The women wanted teachers to teach their children English and they wanted a new school. I did not have the money to build a new school for them. Also, as a teacher I always believed it was the relationship between a teacher and a student that mattered, not the building. So I've been in touch with retired teachers who will respect the faith of my Chinese sisters and go over as volunteers to teach English. Eventually, I want to bring some of those students to Canada on scholarship at the University of Alberta.

I have always felt a strong connection to the children of China; I cannot explain it, but I believe my mission to China was part of a larger plan. The poverty of the 1930s reinforced my faith in the Creator, and the Depression taught me to value the free things in life such as the beauty of nature, trees, birds, wild flowers, and weeds like the dandelion. Today their beautiful yellow carpet lines my country driveway and covers my lawn. It is a challenge to defend their right to exist, to enjoy their brief span of beauty. When my well meaning family reaches for the lawn mower, I am obliged to remind them of their youth; on their way home from school my children would pick a bouquet of dandelions, rush into the house, all three of them trying to be the first to give me their bouquet.

My country home is on a hill, in front of another hill, looking over a wide expanse of valley where the beavers share their pond with the swallows, geese, ducks, loons, and hawks. We all share the little hills and valleys with white-tailed deer, moose, bears, coyote, fox, and the odd wolf. I call this home, but it is God's domain, the largest mosque built by Allah. Each time I turn the key in the lock, I am flooded with joy and peace.

My husband Al built this home, and we had lived in it for about 20 years when he passed away. Long before his death, Al and I dreamed about visiting the great mosques of the world. We were fascinated by the mosques of Spain and the famous Muslims who had fostered knowledge in the arts, the sciences, mathematics, and in the field of medicine. In 1974 Al and I travelled to Spain and prayed in the Great Mosque of Cordoba. The huge columns separating us became a maze, and the light from the opening in the ceiling flooded the floor. When we found each other after the prayer, we were both crying. We were so overwhelmed by the immense spirituality of this holy place. The feeling was indescribable.

Lila Fahlman

Lila Fahlman will publish a book on her life through Purple Wolf Publishing House, Box 128, Seba Beach, Alberta, T0E 2B0.

Solmaz

I spent the first nineteen years of my life in the city of Antep in southern Turkey. My family was well to do, and I had loving parents, grandparents, uncles, aunts, cousins, two younger sisters and a baby brother around me. As the first-born grandchild, I was lavished with attention and thoroughly spoiled. My grandparents lived in our home and there was no concept of a generation gap. Their wisdom and experience bridged the gap between parents and children. They had the time to play games with me, and they were the ones to remind my parents that they were once children, too. Through their stories, my grandparents helped me understand my parents better. My grandparents shared our family histories and gave me a strong sense of who I was. At the same time, my youth kept them in touch with the changing world: new fashions, new books, new songs — they all filtered into the home through me and the other children. Years later — living in Canada — it came as a surprise to me that people considered it unusual for three generations to live together, let alone understand each other.

The rules guiding my life were straightforward. Grown-ups were respected and obeyed without question. This held true not only for family members but also for neighbors and even strangers. It would not be unusual for a stranger to scold a child for breaking a flower or running in the street. Even though I was surrounded by adults who monitored my behavior, my family was still very protective of me. I was not allowed to play outside and rarely allowed to visit friends. My parents preferred to have friends come to our home instead.

Shortly after I completed my education, I was engaged to be married. Fuad was a medical doctor working in a small town outside of Antep. At the time of our engagement he told me he planned to go to the United States for postgraduate studies after practising in Turkey for three more years. Years earlier he had been awarded a Fulbright scholarship to study in the United States, but his parents had been opposed to him leaving Turkey as a young, unmarried man. He was still determined to go to the United States to study about advances in medicine. So before I made the decision to marry him, he wanted me to know that he expected to leave Turkey. I agreed, even though I had never left the country or been away from my family. I was impressed by his idealism and enthusiasm to improve himself, and I wanted to help him realize his dreams. If someone had told me that my decision would dramatically change my life and would permanently take me away from my family and country, I would not have believed it. In the 1950s, airline travel was still a rare event, and the USA was a country at the other end of the world, glimpsed only through movies in a darkened theater. Children grew up, married, and lived their whole lives in the same place.

Fuad and I were married on September 4, 1954, in my hometown of Antep. Our new life together began in a small town where he was working. Three years and two daughters later, we moved to Istanbul where Fuad began his postgraduate studies. At that time, he sent applications to continue his studies at hospitals in the USA and Canada. When Fuad received an acceptance from the Hotel Dieu Hospital in Kingston, Ontario, he chose it over the American hospitals because Canada was bilingual and his French was very good. He also liked the fact that Kingston was located on Lake Ontario. Fuad's father had often told him that given a choice, it's always nicer to live near the seaside. An inland lake seemed like an adequate substitute! Three weeks after the birth of our third daughter, Fuad moved to Kingston and began his training at the Hotel Dieu Hospital. He was paid two hundred dollars a month — not enough to support a family, so the girls and I stayed in Istanbul with my parents.

Solmaz Sahin, Niagara-on-the-Lake, 1998.

The Hotel Dieu was a Catholic hospital run by nuns, and Fuad was the first Muslim doctor at that hospital. The nuns were very kind and respectful of his religious beliefs. They gave him a blanket to use as a prayer rug. Orders were issued to the cafeteria staff to provide him with special food, and in the fasting month of Ramadan, he was given an early meal in the morning and again when he broke his fast in the evening. After a year of internship and a year of residency, Fuad moved to England to continue his surgical training in Liverpool. Less than two months later, the girls and I joined him there. I was filled with mixed emotions — happy to be joining my husband, but sad to be leaving my family and the familiarity of my country.

We lived in England for almost a year. During that time, Fuad received an offer from Dr Killingbeck, a man he had met during his stay in Canada. It was an offer too good to refuse and so in August 1961, we moved to the small town of Hearst in northern Ontario. I often think that Dr Killingbeck played an instrumental role in our lives — it was because of him that we settled in Canada. Otherwise, Fuad would have finished his training in England and we would have likely returned to Turkey.

I had just started to adjust to life in England when we moved to Canada and to a new challenge. In Hearst, most of the population was French-Canadian. My ears, barely accustomed to the English language, were now exposed to French as well. And the English was spoken with a Canadian accent! Even our girls, who had learned English so well in such a short period of time in Liverpool, couldn't understand the Canadian accents.

Hearst was a stark contrast to the big city atmosphere of Liverpool. With its population of barely 2,000, Hearst seemed unusually small and isolated. There were no apartments or any other rental housing so we stayed at Dr Killingbeck's home and waited for a place. We eventually moved into a small house outside of town. Our first months in Hearst introduced us to black flies, and I heard that if a person was tied to a tree, he could die after being exposed to the bites for just two to three hours. There were beautiful forests and small lakes in the area, yet it was impossible to have a picnic outside.

We were rescued from the black flies by the start of winter, a winter so cold and long that to this day I still remember it vividly. The normal temperature was 40 degrees below zero and occasionally it would drop to 60 below! If you tried to open an outside door handle without gloves, your hand would burn from the cold. The snow was very deep and for five months it never melted. The children couldn't be seen behind the snow banks as they walked to and from school. After a few days of worrying about our daughters making their way home from school safely, Fuad had the girls walk the short distance to the hospital after school. They would wait there for him to finish his work and then come home together in the warmth of the car.

For me, the saving grace of those winter months was the sunshine. The brilliance of the sun on that beautiful white

Solmaz Sahin and her daughters, 1964.

snow warmed me inside. The people of Hearst were also very warm and friendly. I started attending English classes two evenings a week at the local high school. I was the only foreigner there; all the other students were French-speaking Canadians. Sometimes it seemed to me that I would learn to speak French before I learned English!

With the change of seasons from winter to spring, Fuad and I were both ready to move. That summer we moved to Kingston where Fuad started his third year of residency. One day Fuad was shocked to hear the children swearing at each other with words they had picked up from other children in the neighborhood. In that instant he turned to me and said, "We're moving." How difficult it was for me to realize that I couldn't understand what my daughters were saying. This was worse than any financial struggle, any loneliness or homesickness — the frustration of confronting how foreign I felt in my own home. It was then I recognized that I was not only a foreigner outside of my home, but also inside it — a place that

Solmaz Sahin and her children, 1970.

should have felt safe and secure. And so in the middle of winter, with the girls halfway through their school year, we moved once again. We were fortunate to find a house for rent right across from the hospital. It was the fourth move in three years. Looking back at it now, I wonder where we found the energy. Fuad was working long hours at the hospital, and I had my hands full raising three children under the age of seven.

My children consumed me day and night. I was so busy I didn't have time to think. It was only when the children didn't need me as much that I began to feel the void and I used to dream of going back to Turkey. When I got frustrated or angry, I would run out into the garden and dig or plant and the physical work would help me. When I complained, my husband would tell me to go to the hospital to see the sick people. This gave me perspective. I believe that as long as I have my health, I have no reason to complain. I had also agreed not to work outside the home. It was not unusual at the time for women to stay home. By the time I did want to do work outside the home, it was probably too late.

In Kingston I met a few Turkish families. We couldn't see each other a lot–lack of transportation — yet we often spoke on the phone. I felt so vulnerable then, struggling with what people were saying on the phone, with reading food labels or notes from school. Sometimes I felt overwhelmed by this foreignness– — radio, television, newspapers, street signs, and billboards. I longed for something familiar! I wondered if I'd ever feel comfortable. I started taking English classes again in the evenings at the local high school. Through these classes I met a wonderful Canadian lady, Mrs Jeannette Capell. She had volunteered through a church organization to help new immigrants practice their English. Once a week, I would go to her house and work on my conversation skills. I was amazed by Mrs Capell's efforts to help newcomers. An elderly widow, she opened her home to as many as twenty strangers at a time and helped us make a connection to this new country. I will never forget her warmth and kindness. We kept in touch with her for many years and it warms my heart to remember her even now.

During our second year in Kingston, Fuad changed his residency to urology and thought that speciality would be needed in a small town. He found a job. Once again with Dr Killingbeck, again in northern Ontario, but this time in Matheson — a town even smaller than Hearst! It boasted a population of 920 people and is situated between Timmins and Kirkland Lake.

Matheson was very English-Canadian, and by then I was able to communicate more comfortably in English and made friends with some of the ladies there. I learned how to curl in Matheson and my friends helped me practice my driving. They were happier than I was when I passed my driver's test! Occasionally I would drive to Timmins, about an hour away, for a change of scenery. There were more shops there, a dry cleaner, and a movie theater. It was there the girls saw *Mary Poppins*, their first movie.

Our girls were growing and we often worried about their religious education. Although we had taught them the basics, we knew they needed more. In Turkey, children are sent to special teachers to learn their religion. Who would teach our children here? Raising children is difficult under the best of circumstances, but for us it was even more difficult. We were unprepared for the influences of a non-Muslim environment on our children, and had little experience to draw on for guidance. Sometimes we were confronted by strangers: our own children! Where did they get certain ideas? They absorbed so much from school, television, and the people around them and these values became such a big part of their lives without us noticing. Once, a long time ago, I believed it was parents who ultimately determined how children would turn out. I am more aware now that children are as much a product of the environment as they are of the influences of their parents. My false impression of the exclusive role of parents was formed in a relatively homogenous society. Everybody had more or less the same set of values. What was taught and practised at home was reinforced by the environment.

Fuad wanted to do an extra year in residence because of the change he had made in his specialization, so we moved to Hamilton. Living there brought important changes to our lives. One day at the hospital, Fuad met a pharmaceutical sales representative named Said Zefer. Fuad learned that he was a Muslim from Pakistan living in Toronto. It was from Said that we learned there was a Muslim community in Toronto. He told us about meetings every Sunday in a building on Dundas Street. For the first time in the six years since we had left Turkey, our children met other Muslim children. They went to religious classes in Toronto on Sundays. The community worked hard to organize the school and fix the building. Most of us were still new immigrants who missed our families and homelands. We shared the loneliness and the worries about our future. Things we never had to consider in our native countries were critical issues for us here. There was no imam licensed to perform a Muslim marriage ceremony that would be recognized by the Canadian government. I also remember how other Canadians found it so unusual when we requested to have a funeral on a Sunday, as Muslims must be buried within 24 hours of death. I wondered who would wash my body for burial if I died in Canada. In Turkey, there was always someone available for such things. During Ramadan, the ladies of the community would prepare the food to break the fast on Sundays. I would cook food at home and bring it to Toronto. People donated money for the dinners to help cover community expenses. For Eid prayers we would rent a hall and spread sheets on the floor. I would praise Allah and try not to think too much of the Eid prayers on Persian rugs in beautiful mosques back home with our relatives.

When we moved to Niagara Falls in the summer of 1966, we were so happy to find another Muslim family there. The woman was a new bride from Turkey, while the husband was a Bosnian. A year later Hasan Karachi and Nimet had their first daughter, Nina. We became very good friends — almost like one family. Nina was almost a sister to our delighted daughters. Fifteen months later, Nadine was born, followed by Ahmet a year later. Our son Mustafa was born four months after Ahmet. These four children were very close and for us parents it was valuable to have family friends who shared our religious values. Our children, who had grown up all these years without grandparents, aunts, uncles and cousins, finally found an extended family and a home that was always open to them.

We continued to take our girls to Toronto for Islamic lessons on Sundays, but after a while they got bored as they were taught the same lessons over and over again. Through two graduate students who taught the classes we became acquainted with a larger number of Muslim students and the Muslim Students Association (MSA). Eventually, the first Canadian MSA Convention was held in 1967 at McMaster University in Hamilton, Ontario. We attended that conference and the next one in Wisconsin, and have been regular attendants since then. At the beginning there were no women in the leadership.

We also became aware of other Muslim communities, particularly in London (Ontario), Montreal, Halifax, and Vancouver. We visited the London community on a few occasions and were impressed with their wonderful spirit. They were mostly Lebanese Muslims led by the late Albert Hassan. Eventually these leaders decided to organize and the Council of Muslim Communities of Canada (CMCC) was founded. Through the CMCC, the Muslim communities got to know each other, co-ordinated activities, interacted with various levels of government, represented Canadian Muslims to the Muslim countries of the world, and entered into dialogue with different Christian organizations.

Fuad was deeply involved with these Muslim organizations and the meetings took him to different cities in Canada, the USA, and overseas. I stayed home with the children. These were difficult times as the CMCC took my husband away during times that should have been our family time. Although I am proud of the important work of Fuad and other Muslim leaders during those pioneering years, I also recognize the many sacrifices made by the families. We women were often the unsung heroes who toiled in the background, cooking for community dinners, and managing our homes and families so that our husbands could do this volunteer work. Our children sacrificed by not being able to spend more time with their father. Everything has a price, so that is how we paid for this work.

I also felt some sorrow in those days because I had not seen my family for eight years. When they came to visit us in 1968, it was as if my children were meeting their grandparents for the very first time. My youngest daughter Leyla was surprised that they were so young, she thought that grandparents were supposed to be old and have gray hair. The following year we returned to Turkey for the first time in nine years and were able to meet other relatives. Those were wonderful times. Leyla once complained that we had no right to raise children without grandparents. Who knows how many times she may have wished to be able to see her grandparents and have them near.

When my father died of cancer at the age of 58, it was very difficult for me. This loss and the thousands of miles that separated us were painful and still are even many years later. In this country, when I was sad, I felt alone, and even when I was happy, I felt alone. My children didn't understand this when I tried to explain it to them. Many years later when Leyla was living in Turkey and a close relative died, she told me that she finally understood what I meant. She saw the support that families gave each other during difficult times.

During these years other Muslim families moved into the area and we started to meet regularly for Friday prayers at the

Karachi home. As her children grew older, Nimet started to take her children to Toronto for the Muslim school until Fuad offered to teach her children with our son, Mustafa. Later on other children joined in and soon there was an Islamic school with classes held regularly at the Karachi home. The Eid prayers were held at our house but as the community grew we needed a larger place. We raised money and bought property and Hasan Karachi put all his energy and resources into building the mosque on Lyons Creek Road.

A very special Islamic community grew in the Niagara area, a community that began to take the place of grandparents, uncles, and aunts. In these years a summer camp was established because the young people needed a place to meet and form friendships. The first camp was held at a farm owned by a Muslim family. In the early days we didn't have the luxury of hiring cooks and caretakers, so the mothers did the cooking, cleaning, and general duties. The first year the kids slept in tents, and eventually we built a mess hall and added cabins. Later we rented a campground and eventually the Muslim community organized to buy property. Now there is a Muslim camp owned by Muslims and run by Muslims. When I visited the camp this past summer, I was so proud to recognize the camp leaders as those who had attended as children.

Although we came to Canada with the intention of just staying three years, we have spent most of our lives here. In 1971 we moved to our present residence near Niagara-on-the-Lake, a very special place. This home has been called "the house of the imam" because there was hardly any Muslim activity that did not start in our home. The Canadian Council of Muslim Women (CCMW), the CMCC, the Islamic camps, and the IDRF Muslim Relief Agency were all launched at various meetings held at this house in Niagara-on-the-Lake. We have hosted Muslim visitors from overseas and have also provided a retreat for board members of other Muslim organizations. Although it is a lot of work for me, I do not regret it. I believe this is a very worthwhile sacrifice of my personal time.

This place is also the most permanent home our children have had. It was here that I experienced many of the challenges of parenting. The children struggled because their names are different. One day our son Mustafa refused to go to hockey tryouts, and we found out later the kids had made fun of his name. His father asked him if he wanted to change his name, but he said no. After a few fights with other kids, the issue was resolved for him and he seemed to adjust. It was also very hard for me when our eldest daughter Selma left home for university. She was only 17 and I feared outside influences on her. Our youngest daughter Leyla was unhappy and did not reach her potential in high school or university. In hindsight, she suffered partly because she attended a school with lower academic standards, she had few friends with similar interests, and she was in a different school from her older sisters (who thrived and were very active in their school). Our son Mustafa benefited from some lessons we learned from Leyla. When he became unhappy in grade school, his marks dropped and he began to get stomachaches. When we investigated, we learned that he was a gifted child who was often bored in school and he was also picked on by a teacher. After we switched him to a different class in another school, he got up on time, his ailments disappeared, and he stopped complaining.

During their teenage years we told our children that as Muslims they were not allowed to date. I know they had a very hard time accepting this, but they didn't say too much. If they had grown up in Turkey, they would not have had this problem. When my children were small, I went to an Islamic meeting in Toronto. At the time I didn't understand the woman who told the gathering in tears how she had lost her three daughters. They had all married non-Muslims because they were never allowed to associate with Muslims. We tell the young people about all they cannot do and we put so much stress on them. I believe this is the greatest stress they feel, and so I wish there were more activities for young people to do together. As a parent it is much harder to walk the middle path than it is to not practice our religion or to be strict. I spent many sleepless nights convinced my children would marry non-Muslims. I shared my fears with close friends. Marriage is difficult, and with no Muslim grandparents it is much harder for the children.

We never pressured our children into marriage. I believe everything is predetermined, Kismit . . . it is written. So, regardless

Solmaz Sahin (center) entertains Malaysian students
during Eid at her home in Niagara-on-the-Lake, 1998.

of what I think, my children will marry who they were meant to marry. Two of my daughters married in their early twenties. Selma married a man from the West Indies. Hulya married a Bosnian and the ceremonies were performed in our home. Shortly after, Hulya decided to wear the hijab. At the beginning I was surprised, but it was her choice. My youngest daughter Leyla is working in Turkey. She decided to go there to work with a friend. As an added bonus she gets to spend a lot of time with her grandmother, aunts, and uncles. She also finds less societal pressure to get married there. My son Mustafa has dual citizenship and recently performed his obligatory military service in Turkey. He is currently living in New York City.

My granddaughter got married at the age of 15 to the son of a dear friend of her father's. At first I thought they'd be engaged for a while and wait until she finished her education, but her future husband didn't want to wait. So, of her own free will, she decided to marry. This child, who was raised in Buffalo, United States, is now living in Turkey. And at the age of nineteen she has the maturity to deal with a new family and a different kind of life. Life is full of surprises. In typical grand-parent style, I say that our other grandchildren have not visited as often as I would like.

Generations of Muslims growing up in Canada today may not be aware of what life was like for the first Muslims here. Like tree and plant cuttings from around the world, we Muslims have established new roots and have enriched this country with religious, cultural, culinary, and racial diversity. But the ties to our roots are strong, and I feel it is important to retain our native language and the good aspects of our culture and rituals. Most of us had no intention of being pioneers of new Muslim communities, nor did we have a grand plan. We simply discovered that part of the secret of a good life is a strong community of faith. So in bits and pieces we did what was necessary. The discrimination and tension along the way is natural when foreign cultures are brought together, yet I believe non-Muslims have less ignorance and fear after opportunities to interact with Muslims. Two years ago I was pleasantly surprised to read an article about Ramadan and Eid in *Chatelaine*, a prominent Canadian women's magazine. Yet I have not forgotten what happened to the Italians, the Chinese, the Japanese, and many others. Those people were demonized by the Canadian government and some were interned, others had to pay a head tax to get into Canada. We are all guests in this country and for the most part Canada has been a generous host. I have also learned from non-Muslims and have increased my understanding and tolerance of differences.

Sometimes I complain about being here. I am the only one in my family who left my country, and when I left I thought it was temporary. I didn't have to leave Turkey for a better life. I left a life that was easy for me as a Muslim for one that has been much more difficult. One day when I was complaining, a family friend said those who leave are special people with a vision chosen by God. Living in a Muslim country I may not have felt the need to serve Allah as much. Here I was given the opportunity to serve Him better. Perhaps this was my mission.

Solmaz Sahin

Atiya

In the world today, thousands of people migrate from one location to another, and over 200,000 new immigrants come into Canada each year. This migration occurs for many different reasons. In our tradition, we have the example of Prophets Abraham and Moses who migrated and led their people to safety and liberty. Our Prophet Muhammad, peace be upon him, along with his family and friends, also migrated from Mecca to Medina to escape from his enemies.

Migration is often necessary to escape religious, racial, linguistic, or cultural persecution. People also look for political security, to escape situations where unnecessary bloodshed, rioting, and general civil unrest are common. Most of us seek better lives for our children and ourselves so we search for new lands. It was in this pursuit that my family left our home in Pakistan.

My husband and I had a difference of opinion about migrating to the West. For over ten years we debated back and forth about the merits of staying in Pakistan or immigrating to North America. My husband had been overseas several times to pursue higher education. He had studied in the United States and Europe while I stayed with my children in an extended family with my in-laws in Karachi. Perhaps because of my young years and the familiarity and security of a warm family, the thought of leaving it all behind frightened me.

During the presidential election in the early 1960s, the political unrest, senseless killings, and violence became unbearable.

One day on my way to see relatives, my children and I saw students rioting. Some people were attacked and probably killed. I was very worried about the children being exposed to violence. At the time my husband was working in Canada, so for the well-being of my children, I thought it best to build our lives elsewhere and join my husband. So, in search of peace, freedom and a better future for our children, we decided to make Canada our new home. In hindsight, I've realized I can never escape political violence because I see it day to day on television and in the newspapers. Nevertheless, we sought a safe haven in the most peaceful country in the world by far.

Our friends and family came to the airport to see us off, including my maternal uncle. My father had passed away long ago and mother had died three years before I left. I was very close to my maternal uncle as he was both mother and father to me. He was very sad to see us leave the country and him, I still remember his face. He passed away two years later. I was totally devastated and to this day I cannot speak about him without tears.

My three children and I spent one week in London with my sister where we purchased clothing we thought suitable for Canadian winters. We arrived in Canada on February 25, 1965. As it happened, our arrival in this winter wonderland was accompanied by a formidable blizzard that descended upon southern Ontario as our plane was scheduled to land in Toronto. Our flight was diverted to Montreal. Upon landing, the immigration formalities seemed to last forever and appeared all the more difficult because of our unfamiliarity with the French language. When my two daughters, my son, and I came out of the airport to board the train from Dorval to Toronto, the scene was something to behold. I had never experienced such a biting wind, the blowing snow, and the bone-chilling cold. Every step we took filled our boots with more and more snow and the chill became numbing. We had never seen snow before and to see it in such abundance was overwhelming.

Our challenges in a new country began as we set foot in the snow; we were in for many tests in our adopted homeland. With our carry-on luggage in our hands, slipping and sliding,

Atiya Jafri, 1960, Pakistan.

we boarded the train and stayed close to the washroom throughout our journey, still reeling from airsickness. Our train was very crowded and there was absolutely no place to sit. We took turns sitting and kneeling whenever possible. The train journey finally ended and we arrived at Toronto's Union Station at approximately 1:00 a.m. The joy of seeing a familiar face, that of my husband, cheered us all up immensely.

Front Street was covered with snow, quiet yet stormy. We stood on the sidewalk to hail a cab, but to no avail. My husband decided that it was as good a time as any to acquaint us with Toronto's subway system. We boarded the last subway train of the night, and from Museum station we covered a short distance on foot. But this trek was difficult and we were glad to finally get a cab. Our new home was Mayfair Mansions,

*Atiya Jafri's children play in the snow
the day after they arrive in Canada, 1965.*

where we enjoyed the luxury of a maid service and had kitchen facilities. But unlike in Pakistan, there were no servants to cook the meals.

The next day, once again on foot, we went grocery shopping. The snow had stopped but it was bitterly cold. My first experience in a Canadian grocery store is still a vivid memory. In Pakistan, staples such as flour, sugar, rice, oil, lentils, tea, and spices were bought in bulk to last at least a month. Meat, vegetables, eggs, dairy products, and bread were purchased daily by the hired help. This shopping trip was distinctly different. Searching for each and every item and filling a shopping cart by myself was a new experience. Spices were only available in tiny bottles. Coming from a culture where spices are used abundantly, we used to run out of this commodity very quickly and the food often tasted bland.

Another dilemma was whether or not to eat meat. In Karachi, before leaving for Canada, I had consulted with the foremost religious authority. He had advised that it was permissible to eat halal meat from a Muslim butcher, and if that was not available, kosher meat from a Jewish butcher would be all right. And if kosher meat was not available either, then meat from any Christian butcher would be fine. At the beginning, we could not find halal or kosher. We had to make do with meat from Loblaws. Finally, we discovered Kensington Market and a few excellent kosher shops. We would order kosher meat from our favorite shops and the problem was solved when halal meat shops started to spring up in Toronto in the early 1970s.

Coming from a country where I was surrounded by family, I had never been alone in a house. I was terrified when the children went off to school and my husband to work. But somehow I got over the fear and slowly adjusted.

I used to get around in my sari and found it to be quite a challenge because women in saris were a rare sight on Toronto streets in 1965. The stares, jabs, and taunts were both humiliating and awkward because I didn't feel comfortable addressing them. Being a woman from a culture in which women generally did not assert their presence, I would grin and bear it.

As Mayfair Mansions was an apartment hotel, we could not afford its luxuries on a long-term basis and found an apartment in the emerging planned community of Thorncliffe Park. There, the children attended a new school, and because of the gift children have for resilience, they adjusted well to this new school. Even though they had separated from their relatives and friends in Pakistan, they continued to accept and adapt to their new circumstances very well. The two youngest children soon gained excellent command of the English language in a very short time. There were no English as a Second Language classes at the time in the Toronto school system. My eldest daughter, who had been attending an English-medium school (a school where all of the subjects are taught in English) in Karachi, was asked to attend an extra half-hour of remedial English. This did not last very long and she soon began to top her class in English grammar.

When we first began to search for apartments for the family, we noticed many "adults only" signs. This concept of isolating different age groups, particularly children and seniors, seemed very odd to me because I came from an extended family. After being here for a few short weeks, we began to meet Muslim families of Indian and Pakistani origin. They helped us adjust to the new culture and 'the Canadian way' of doing things. They were always willing to take us sightseeing and introduced us to others from our background. Our social life with our new friends became very busy. We were soon going on picnics, and dinner parties, and celebrating Eid and other important Muslim traditions with them. Those early friendships have been lasting ones and we continue to have a special bond with many of these families.

Over time, the number of people like ourselves continued to grow and our circle of friends grew into a community. Like all other communities, we began to experience differences of opinion. The degree to which women should be covered, dietary restrictions, and the way children should be raised became contentious issues. I believed the best way to resolve these differences was by respecting each other's feelings and opinions. Consensus building aside, being intransigent and belligerent only leads to bad feelings and is very unproductive and discouraging. We cannot force our opinions on others, nor do we want to be forced to accept others' opinions without wholesome discussion.

Even my husband and I have two different views of Islam. He believes in it on a philosophical level but does not feel it necessary to pray five times a day, fast, or go on pilgrimage. I, however, do not believe you can separate the religious obligations from the philosophy. Although my husband appears very enlightened from a religious point of view, he was very traditional in other ways. When I wanted to learn how to drive, he was afraid I'd have an accident. As I got older and wanted to go out, he was concerned about ice and snow in the winter and sun and heat in the summer. He never worries about the younger women in the family in this way so I can only attribute this behavior to the society where he grew up where women needed to be protected.

In this country I had total freedom of religion and was able to practice my faith without any restrictions. I believe that as far as my faith is concerned, it is a personal matter and no

Atiya Jafri with her husband and daughter, 1967.

Atiya Jafri gives a birthday party, 1967.

one has the right to interfere with it in any way. I also believe
that criticizing other faiths and religious practices is inappro-
priate and uncivilized. Before coming here, I was unaware of
other people's customs and traditions. In fact, my knowledge
was somewhat limited and misguided. Knowing and understanding people of different faiths and backgrounds has been a
very rewarding and enriching experience.

When we first arrived, several of our Canadian acquaintances
extended a hand of friendship towards our family, and my husband's colleagues at the office invited us for tea or dinner so that
we would feel at home in our new country. They tried to help us
in any way they could. For our part, we tried to acquaint them
with our customs and habits, particularly on the subject of food
and drink. They respected our religious dietary requirements
and were happy not to serve us alcoholic beverages or serve ham
and pork products.

When I went to look for a job, I was advised that I would
have better luck if I dressed in 'Canadian' clothes for my job
interviews. I was also getting tired of stares and questions
about my sari: How many yards is this gown made of? Don't
you find it hard to walk in that outfit? Don't you feel cold? I
was tired of putting on a phony smile. The truth of the matter
was that snow and salt were ruining my saris and my legs also
felt the cold in the winter. Because of these reasons, despite
some uneasiness, I decided to wear skirts and dresses to work.
Luckily, after a year or two, because the social climate was
changing for women, pant suits were in vogue. The dress code
at the office also changed and my dress problem was solved. I
enjoyed wearing trendy pant suits because they resembled *shal-
war/qameez* suits and were far more comfortable than any
other form of clothing. Of course, the men did not have to
struggle with what to wear because they wore business suits to
the office in Pakistan and continued to wear them here. Even
casual clothing for men consisted of pants and shirts and there
was no question of modesty or exposed skin.

The curiosity of strangers was endless. Where are you
from? Why don't you have a Pakistani accent when you speak
English? Most Indians and Pakistanis have skinny arms and
legs, how come yours aren't? Your children must have had to

Atiya Jafri with her daughters, 1999.

sit on mats at school; they probably haven't seen desks before. How long did you live here for your skin to become light? Because of my light skin, people often denied me my background. Once in a grocery store two older women had a conversation about me: "These men come over and marry our women." It was clear that I did not fit the stereotypical view of Pakistani women and this was brought home to me time and again. The comments and questions were often hurtful, but it was up to me to correct the perceptions and respond with dignity. Once I went for a job interview and the employer thought that I was from Palestine instead of Pakistan. He ended the interview right away and told me that the job had already been filled and there were no more openings. I can only assume that because of my light skin, he thought I was Arab instead of South Asian. Besides, in the 1960s, few people had heard of Pakistan.

When the children were in school, I read one of their books, *The Stone Angel* by Margaret Laurence. The struggles faced by the main character mirrored many of my own struggles in adjusting to a new life. I identified so much with this truly Canadian character that I obtained permission to translate the book into Urdu and I plan to publish it myself.

I believe my struggles were nothing compared to those of my children. The children were constantly asked awkward questions because they were different. They always had to come up with their own answers. My daughters had to contend with the issue of dating during their teenage years and were no doubt under tremendous peer pressure. The difficulties they had to face in view of this pressure only they know and can explain. At home they were being instructed on what was right or wrong in our own culture. To this day, I wonder how they dealt with these conflicting pressures.

Luckily they enjoyed the company of compassionate friends. Many of their friends were non-Muslim and non-South Asian because those communities were not very large. Today at work they encounter people from a broad range of backgrounds, a gift they enjoy in the Canadian workplace. And there is also a large extended family of cousins, aunts, and uncles all over North America. I believe my children are a product of both the East and the West and their traditional values mesh well with this modern and generous country.

My children eventually got married, but for the first time in our family, one of those marriages ended in divorce. I didn't know how to cope with this situation. My daughter's husband was a very religious man and we were close to him so we were very unprepared. They had a daughter when he left and that little girl was very close to her father. I can't explain the pain of watching my granddaughter adjust to life without him. I don't think I will ever forget what she went through.

My grandson also has a visual impairment and that has hit the family very hard. We first noticed it when he was about three months old. His eyes did not follow anything put in front of him. Would his sight improve over time or would it deteriorate? Would he ever lead a normal life? The entire family struggled hard with these questions. Thank God, now at the age of nine, his sight is much better than it was.

Although the birth of my five grandchildren has filled me with joy and anticipation, I worry about my grandchildren. The children of today are faced with many challenges and bombarded with conflicting values. I hope they are able to meet sincere and caring people in their lives who will support them through the good and bad times.

Finally, I would like to share some wisdom with the younger sisters. You are all responsible for the success of our community and your ambition, intelligence, and common sense will pave the way for the future. You have the opportunity to reflect on our traditional values and benefit from them. I believe strongly in the Islamic concept of justice; to learn to respect all human beings, regardless of their circumstances. And to strive for simplicity and knowledge. You also have the opportunity to evaluate the strengths and weaknesses of this culture. I like the notion of defining a goal, working hard for it, but also taking personal responsibility for attaining it. You will choose the best of both worlds.

Atiya Jafri

*This story was translated from Urdu to English
by Atiya's daughter, Nuzhat Jafri.*

Mariam

I am French-Canadian, brought up in a very small town in eastern Quebec. We moved to Ontario when I was 15 years old, to Brampton, which was then a very small town compared to what it is today. When we moved to Ontario I became exposed to other religions. Where I was brought up there was one religion — Catholic. I was a very strong practising Catholic: in the 1950s in Quebec, well, you had to be. I went to convent school from grade one to grade ten, but I did have a lot of questions inside about my own faith and I could not find any answers. First I looked into Judaism. When I was 16, I got a job with a Jewish family as a babysitter. I thought, maybe, Judaism had more answers than Christianity, but I didn't find anything there. I continued in my search until I met my husband and he told me he was Muslim and I said, "What is that?" I had never heard of Islam. My mother kept referring to him as a Hindu because he was Indian so he had to be Hindu!

My husband Mohamed told me that I did not have to become a Muslim. As a result one of his aunts wrote to him and said, "Don't ever come into my house again!" I didn't know any of his family. But we got married, and on the same day, we had two ceremonies, the Catholic in the morning at church, and in the evening, the Islamic ceremony. So my father made the comment that now I was really married, twice, in front of God. My mother, well, I don't know how she felt. And here we are 28 years later.

Mariam Bhabha (far right, front), rural Quebec, 1956.

I started leaning about Islam — what was it, how did it come about — nothing about the doctrines at first. There was something that kind of appealed to me there, and then I started looking into the doctrines and into the Prophet's life. The last thing I looked into was the Qur'an. That was a four-year search. My big fear was that on the Day of Judgment how would I face God? I had been brought up to think that only the Catholics go to heaven; that was what I was taught by the nuns. Catholics go to heaven because we have a mark; we are baptized and everyone else goes to hell. These were some of the big issues that were going on in my mind even though I was an adult. When I come in front of God how would I explain that I am now a Muslim?

At the time that I became a Muslim I did not wear a hijab (head scarf). That became an issue later on, and I started wearing it about ten years ago. The hijab for me was a way of exposing my Islam, because without it, I am just any Canadian. When I go outside people can say, "Oh there is one of them. Here is a Muslim woman." That was the reason.

My siblings were very supportive; they always supported me in everything. But my mom and dad, it was very hard for them. I was the first in the family to go out of the Catholic faith and it was okay as long as I was quiet about it and nobody knew. The fact that I come from a very traditional family and society, it was and still is difficult. Every time I meet with my parents, my mother, especially, looks at me. "That thing on your head." She doesn't say anything anymore. One comment my father did make to my younger brother was, "Couldn't she wait until we were dead." And that kind of bothered me, but I decided I was going to continue doing my own thing. That is my problem, I am stubborn and I think it is being French-Canadian. The English did that to us! So when I set something in my mind and I say this is the right thing to do, nobody will stop me.

I have been told to go to back where I came from: "Can't you dress Canadian?" The first time it happened it bothered me, I was literally shaking from this older woman telling me how to dress like a Canadian with her very thick English accent. That was the worst thing — who is she to tell me? I am a 17th-generation Canadian! I tell people I have been here much longer than you have. Older people have said, "All these immigrants are here to take our jobs."

I turn around and say, "Why don't you go back to where you came from?"

They say, "Well I was born here."

I say, "What about your father, was he was born here? What about your grandfather?"

With most of them it ends at their grandfather. I find I have to reply in a rather aggressive manner, but in a soft tone of voice to make them realize they are also immigrants. We all came here from somewhere, except for our native peoples.

The Qur'an tells us, to me my religion, and to you, yours. I respect that. I have two children, a boy and a girl. My kids knew they were Muslim from the day they were born. They have gone through the Islamic Sunday school. They were brought up in an environment that was mostly made up of non-Muslims and they know that when they go to my mother's house there is the crucifix and there are the pictures because grandma is Christian. Then they go to the other side of the family, this is the Muslim family, they knew by the home. But I have never imposed anything on them, including the hijab on my daughter. I always told my son when he was six or so, he loved pasta — spaghetti and macaroni — he used to say he was going to marry an Italian girl. I have always told him that he could marry a non-Muslim if he wanted. Who am I to tell him who he cannot marry? His father married me! But I would work very hard on her to make her a Muslim. My daughter used to say, "How come I cannot marry a non-Muslim?" And when she was four she objected to wearing a scarf to pray because her brother was not wearing a scarf and that was not fair. What can I say? These are things you just have to accept. That is the way life is.

Had I not become a Muslim, then the war in Bosnia would not have affected me as much as it did. Also my children were older when it happened. Ten years earlier, if Bosnia had happened, I don't know if I would have had the time to get involved at the level that I did. Secondly, Bosnian Muslims are European like I am, so I did find a bit of a kinship. When I had become a Muslim many years ago, within the circle that I moved, I was always the only white Muslim. I did not know there were European Muslims. When the war broke out, my first question to my husband was, "Where is this Bosnia?" So he gave me a short history lesson. I did some reading myself about Bosnia and the Bosnian people.

When the war broke out, the Muslim Yugoslav population here in southern Ontario was very small. So myself, and two other women, one a lawyer, created the Bosnian-Canadian Relief Association. Within days we got charitable status and we started working right away. We collected over 60 containers of things like clothes, medical supplies, and food through the organization. I was a volunteer and I never took a penny, even phone calls I made from home. I felt that was my way to repay society.

I was getting more and more into it without realizing it. This is what I have to do. One day my husband said to me, "What do you think? That you are going to change the world?"

And I looked at him and I said, "Why not? Why not? Maybe I can make a difference?"

It was hard, it took so much out of me. I was heavily

*Bosnian children in school at a refugee camp
near Split, Croatia, 1993.*

involved for two and a half years. It drained me totally — it has taken me another two years to get back on my feet. Thank God the Kosovo war did not happen right after the Bosnian war because I was so emotionally drained.

It was a difficult time for me with my family. I did not always get the support that I thought I should be getting. Who cares about having dinner ready on time when people are dying? I went four times to Bosnia during the war. To go off like that during the war was also difficult on my family. However, at the time, I felt that I had raised my children and they were adults and I was needed more there.

What did I do in Bosnia? First of all, to be a visible Muslim woman present there in the refugee camp was important. If someone had told me that, I would have said, how can that be? It is very difficult to express it in words, but when you go into a camp and you have three, four hundred women in a camp, young girls and older people (all the men are over 65), and they just come running when they see you coming and there you are with your hijab. I always tried to really dress in a long flowing robe whenever I went to Bosnia so I would be really seen as Muslim. I didn't want there to be any confusion because the Orthodox Christian women also wear scarves, as do some of the old Croatian women. I really wanted the Bosnians to know who

Mariam Bhabha at the Zagreb Airport, 1992.

I was. The women you see just come running and they embrace you and then say *salaam alaikum*. That was very important because in that Muslim greeting there was hope for them. Many of the Bosnians I met felt they had been abandoned by the West, and by the world. I was a tiny ray of hope.

In one camp I remember I was sitting with a group of women on the ground and we were having coffee and a bus drove through the camp and there were Japanese or Korean people on the bus. They were possible donors who wanted to see a refugee camp and so the relief agencies organized these tours for them. The translator told me the Bosnian women were saying: "Oh there is another bus of these people coming to look at us like we are monkeys in a zoo."

The first time I went to make contacts because I would eventually be taking material goods and money that were raised here in Canada. I would go into a camp and meet, first of all, with the camp director. It was always a man and a local person. I would get all the figures on how many men, how many women, how many children. Do the kids go to school? Why not?

On my second trip I had seven extra pieces of luggage that the airline didn't charge me for. These were bales of clothing and each weighed 30 kilos, mostly underwear, and the long skirts the Bosnian women wear. So I took those things and I distributed them to women in the camps. The women had fled their homes so quickly that they didn't have any extra clothes. Imagine having one pair of underwear and you are stuck with that! So I got a group of women in Toronto to go to the Bi-way and buy underwear. Of course, this was with money that was collected here by the Muslim community across Canada. In the camps the women told me they needed sanitary napkins. I went back to the camp director and told him and he was all flustered! "Oh sorry, Allah has created us that way!" Off I went and bought, through a wholesaler, and the women were very happy.

Most of the camps in Croatia were in old Yugoslav army barracks. There would be one room per family and sometimes there were two women and two or three children in one room and they would have mattresses on the floor. When you went into the barracks, there would be a long hallway with rooms on both sides and at the door outside of the hallway would be the shoes, all lined up. Muslims do not wear shoes inside. The camp director would take me and meet the women, and then I would ask for the Bula. She is a woman who wears a hijab and she is respected in the community and is a teacher of the Qur'an. In every camp there was one or two of these women. I would find out from the Bula if they had Islamic classes in the camps. At the beginning of the war most camps didn't; the refugees thought they'd only be in the camp for two or three days. By my third and fourth trip they had regular classes. Another thing I took was books and pictures to put on the walls.

There were social problems in the camps. Some of the young girls coming from small villages, who were now in these camps on the outskirts of big cities, wanted to go out and be teenagers. Their mothers were worried. The local men would also come to the camps looking for girls. Another problem was drugs. Some of the young men from remote areas in the mountains were exposed to drugs and alcohol for the first time in the camps. I would sit with a group of women, and even the camp director, and try to figure out how we should solve these problems. They really wanted to know how to make things better for themselves. I would go back to these camps on different visits and I would ask, "How are things, are they getting better?" I would find some of the same people and some new people. I would be looking for so and so and be told she has gone to Belgium or Sweden.

I took great risk, which I don't regret, but sometimes I wonder, how did I do this? The big stress in Croatia was crossing the border into Bosnia. Somehow, I always got a UNHCR (United Nations High Commission for Refugees) issued blue travel card. With a blue card you could move but then when you get to the Bosnian border point, they search you. Even at the border they never ever searched my bags or asked me for anything. When I took the United Nations plane from Zagreb to Sarajevo, I had a lot of money in my bag and lots of letters from the Bosnian community in Toronto, and seeds for gardens. There was no mail going back and forth. The UN had been confiscating mail: if the Serbs and Croats living in Sarajevo couldn't get mail, then the Bosnians would have to do without mail as well. I had over 100 letters on me. When I went to board the plane, the officer there looked at me, and asked me if I was Muslim.

I said, "Yes."

He said, "So am I, Malaysian," and he just waved me through. My knees were shaking and I felt the stress of carrying all that money and those letters.

When I arrived in Sarajevo, I had to go by a Serb checkpoint and I was really scared because that was shortly after the Serbs had killed the Bosnian deputy Prime Minister. They also tell you on the plane that they cannot protect you if you are taken hostage. I met some Egyptian soldiers at the airport in Sarajevo and they asked me what I was doing there. I said I had to get into the city and they talked and they talked and finally they said they would take me. That is how I got into Sarajevo. I asked about the Serb checkpoint and they said it was okay because I was going in a UN convoy. They zoomed past the checkpoint. Had I been in a private car, I would have been stopped. I made it to the city and distributed all the money to the different relief organizations. I never lost a penny. I always distributed everything that I had. If there was a sick child in a camp, I would give her 100 Deutschmarks, in case she needs an eye examination or medicine.

I remember — funny now when I think about it — travelling over the Atlantic, I was always thinking of strategies. I would have money strapped to me. One time coming out of Bosnia I had pictures of some Muslim units that the Croats had declared war criminals. I was told they could have thrown me in jail for having those photos. I had put the photos in my underwear. I was shaking at the airport and at border crossings

I had to do some pretty difficult things. I had to walk in the tunnel under the Sarajevo airport — there was a hand-dug tunnel that the Bosnians used because they would have been shot on top. I am five foot tall and I had to walk with my head down, all 850 meters. I have a real problem with rodents. I was scared. This was shortly after a friend of mine died here in Canada of cancer, and walking through the tunnel and smelling the earth, and I was in water up to my ankles and I was thinking of my friend in her grave. Anything could have happened, the tunnel could have collapsed, but I made it out. I had to come back the same way and that was very difficult because I also had to carry the bags on my back. I also had to go up and down mountains in jeeps on man-made roads because the main roads could not be used. The terrain was very tough. So when I returned home, physically I was tired, also psychologically tired. It would take me a week to feel normal again.

The worst thing was there was no food over there. When I went to Sarajevo, I literally lived on bread. I had taken a few things with me to share with people. When I came out of Sarajevo and returned to Zagreb, the woman I was staying with made a big meal for me. Physically I was sick. I just couldn't eat. And then coming home and going to the supermarket, I just couldn't do it! There was a time when my family had to take over the grocery shopping, the choice was just too overwhelming.

At home I was getting a lot of flack from Muslim brothers and sisters. "What do you think you are doing, you are just a woman?" One woman, a close friend, said, "It is a man's world out there. What do you think you are doing? Why do you want to go there?"

That was hard, when you have a sister telling you that. It

Mariam Bhabha and her husband and two children.
Woman at far left is a family friend, 1995.

put a little bit of doubt in me, maybe she is right. But then, before very trip I would ask God to give me a little sign — if I am not meant to go, break a leg or something. It never happened, so I would get on the plane and say, "You didn't give me a sign, so don't give me a sign now! Don't crash the plane over the Atlantic. Just take me safely through this journey." Some people said I couldn't travel alone as a woman. I said, "I am not travelling alone, I am with God." I did lose a close friend over this, a Muslim woman. I thought, I have to be able to go to sleep at night and get up in the morning and to look at this face and live with myself. If I can't live with myself, how will I face God on the Day of Judgment? I am accountable for every penny, for every promise I made to help those people.

One time my husband had accepted a dinner invitation the day after I returned.

I said, "No, I am not going." I always wanted to be on my own for about a week, I didn't want to talk to anybody.

He said, "No, you are coming, you have to come."

I went and I was sitting there and he said, "You look so miserable."

"These people are so petty," I said. "How can they complain about this and that when they don't know what is going on in the world?"

He kind of brought me back to earth when he said, "Well you can't blame them for that, this is life here, they don't understand what you have seen on the other side."

And that is how I felt sometimes when talking to people and they would ask, "Why are you doing that and why do you go?" I stopped trying to explain it.

Over the last two years myself and four other women created a women's organization called The Federation of Muslim Women, and one of the things in our mandate is to help women locally and also at an international level. When this Kosovo disaster came about, we had to do something. We joined the task force on Kosovo that was created in Toronto. We said that we would put together one container. Now it is on its way to Albania where the goods will be distributed to the refugees. I found it easier this time because I knew they needed underwear and sanitary napkins.

The trips that I took, the first one was paid by a doctor, the second by my mother-in-law, the third and the fourth were covered by a donor. One thing that hurts me very much is that some people said I was using the money that should go to the refugees. Another thing that people don't seem to realize is that if you collect $100,000, and the money is sitting here in the bank, wouldn't it be better to take $1000 and send someone there with the money so at least it can be used. This is where at times I was at odds with some of the men in the community; they thought women just couldn't do anything right. I always felt a great responsibility to the donor. When people give something, it gives them peace of mind because they made their donation. And in the meantime, the money is sitting here!

It is a hard struggle, we have to educate our men — our Muslim men — before we start pointing fingers at others. I say, let's start looking at ourselves — at times I have not had support from the Muslim community — support I thought I should have had. That was only because I was a woman — because a man who wanted to do what I was doing — the response would be, "Oh fantastic." But for a woman, they say, "You go for hajj, that is your contribution." I went ahead and did what I did because I felt that I was within my rights as a Muslim woman, that it would help other Muslim women.

I was very naïve when I first got involved with the Bosnian issue — naïve in terms of my dealing with people. I always took people at face value. Now I have learned that good people can be nice to you up front, but they'll stab you in the back. I think that I am cautious now. Sometimes I have been sitting in board meetings with a group of people, or maybe talking about strategies, and the next thing you hear — oh this group is doing this. We were going to do it, but someone else stole the ideas. Things like that used to really hurt me.

You know what renewed my faith in people, though? When Nelson Mandela came out of jail — that affected me — I thought he would never get out. My husband is from South Africa and when Mandela came out of jail I thought there is hope, there is hope for this world.

I have seen so much even in Bosnia. War brings out the worst in some people and unfortunately it happened in Bosnia and it is happening in Kosovo now. The black market is flourishing; people just want to make a buck at the expense of others.

I want to tell you something. I just came back from Pakistan and India, and in India I met a young girl about 12 years old with very good English. She was all excited to meet people from Canada. I asked the little girl, "What do you want to be when you grow up?"

And she said, ""I want to be a doctor and I want to be like Mother Teresa."

And I thought, great, this is wonderful. Going back to our hotel that night my husband said to me, "Isn't it sad that she is using Mother Teresa as a figurehead?"

I said, "Well no, why?"

He said, "We don't have a Muslim female role model."

It is true, we do not have someone to look up to, the only women we have are Aisha, and Khaadija, the prophet's wives,

*Mariam Bhabha and her daughter at her university graduation
at Queen's University in Kingston, Ontario, 1998.*

and his daughter Fatima. But we are detached from these women because they are part of history. We need women who can be role models today, in this day and age.

But young Muslim women today really have it easy because there are all kinds of institutions set up to help them out. At the universities, the Muslim Student Associations are active and there are more and more young women on campuses wearing the hijab. It has become more acceptable. Although each generation has its own challenges, I think Canada is the best country to be in if you are a Muslim. I think as Muslim women we are very fortunate to be here. As a Canadian Muslim, this is my country, this is where I belong and I am very proud — very happy, to be living here because under the laws of the land I can practice Islam. I can live Islam. I hope this story will give my daughter a sense of belonging. And maybe one day my granddaughters. We do belong to Canada, all of us.

Mariam Bhabha

Adeena

Growing up in Afghanistan I had a very happy life; I considered myself to be one of the most lucky people in the world. I had good parents, and I got a job I really loved. I started teaching at Kabul University, and then I got a scholarship through a cultural exchange program to go to India to learn Sanskrit.

In India my happy life ended. There was a coup in Afghanistan by the Communist regime. It was organized in the Soviet Union and then, shortly after, the Soviets occupied my country. I was a young, proud woman hoping to go back to Afghanistan to continue my teaching job at the university. The most difficult period of my life was when my country was occupied. When I heard about the coup, my whole family was in Afghanistan, and I knew they wouldn't be indifferent to what was happening. I heard the news on the radio. When I was young, I was very proud so I didn't want to cry in front of anyone. I was living in university residence and I used to lock myself in my room and cry all day. It was as if my life had ended.

With the coup I had become a refugee. The Indian government was not accepting Afghan refugees so I had to claim refugee status at the United Nation High Commission for Refugees (UNHCR). At that time my perception of refugees was far from reality. I felt really ashamed for being a refugee. I felt I had lost everything, my culture, my family, my country, everything.

I got involved in the liberation struggle of my country. I tried to raise awareness in India of how my country had become the victim in a struggle between the Soviets and the Americans.

*Adeena Niazi with her mother,
Kabul, Afghanistan, early 1960s.*

India had a very important status in the region, so I started holding conferences and demonstrations. We also had a student's union that was raising the voice of the Afghans.

I also started working at UNHCR to assist fellow Afghan refugees. It was risky because the Communist government was really tough on the people who raised their voices against them. It was risky because I had my family in Afghanistan, it was risky for me also because I was living on my own. In Afghanistan my sister was arrested and my brother also got into trouble. My friends were warning me. But I had to take risks — the struggle was very important to me.

My perceptions of being a refugee also began to change with my struggle for liberation. I came to feel very differently about myself as a refugee. I realized that it was not my fault and no one wanted to be a refugee. I felt refugees should be proud of standing up for their rights and principles. That gave me more strength.

I kept hoping that things would change, that I would be able to go back to my country. I waited for a decade and then I realized that I couldn't stay in India for long because the relationship between the Indian government and the former Soviet Union was friendly. I could be kicked out at any time, so I claimed refugee status with the Canadian High Commission in New Delhi and I was accepted. I chose Canada because Canada was a land of immigrants.

After I came to Canada, the former Soviet Union was defeated and withdrew from Afghanistan. Subsequently, the Communist regime collapsed and the Western countries lost interest in Afghanistan. Regional powers like Pakistan and Iran began to support and fund different political parties to push their interests in Afghanistan. The struggle for liberation turned into a struggle between different political parties. When the civil war started, Afghanistan was no longer in the news in Western countries. Women in Afghanistan who had already experienced torture, persecution, and violations against their physical dignity during the Soviet installed regime continued to be the victims. Things happened, like rape, that were completely contradictory to the Afghan culture. Women were used as spoils of war, but there was no media attention. Rival warlords were involved in kidnappings and gang rapes. The warlords

*Adeena Niazi (front, second from right)
with her classmates in Kabul, 1975.*

*Adeena Niazi demonstrating in New Delhi, India
against the Soviet occupation, 1985.*

used the rape of women as a reward for their victory over their enemies. I heard of women who committed suicide so they would not be violated. One of my friends told me she heard the daughter of a neighbor screaming in her own house and no one went to help her.

In 1996 the Taliban took over the country and the rapes almost stopped, and some sense of order was restored. But another type of persecution began. New restrictions were imposed on women, and they were now deprived of the right to an education and to work. Women were stoned in front of family members for having relationships outside of marriage. All of a sudden the media paid attention, but the problem had been there for a long time and I had been following the human rights violations. So when the Taliban took over it was not a shock for me; I was very aware of the atrocities that had happened over the past two decades.

When I left Afghanistan, women had enjoyed the same rights as men. Under the Afghani constitution women could become members of parliament, and in some ridings it was a majority of male constituents who elected women to represent them in parliament. Now twenty years later, the sons of those fathers who had elected women as representatives in parliament are chaining women to their homes and depriving them of their basic Islamic and human rights to education and work. The misconception of this political movement as a religious or cultural issue by Western media really breaks my heart. It upsets me very much when the Taliban misrepresent Islam for their own political aims. After all, it was this same country with the same religion and culture that had given women all those rights and respect twenty years ago.

When I came here in 1988, there was an Afghani organization and I joined the board as a member. Although the association provided good services, women were not involved unless there was a celebration and they would cook. They were not part of the decision making. I formed a women's group called the Afghan Women's Organization and incorporated it. I am the volunteer president. It is growing now and is very successful. The Taliban actually helped my work because the world paid attention. Afghanistan came into the world media again and the voices of women were raised.

My country receives plenty of arms but little aid that helps the women and children. In Afghanistan my organization has some relief assistance projects, and we have established three educational classes for girls between eight and 12. Many of these children spend their lives on the street doing nothing. We did some sewing projects where women make crafts that will be sold in their own market in Kabul. We also distribute relief funds to eligible women. In the Afghani refugee camps in Pakistan last year we had a sewing embroidery project. This year we started a chicken-raising project. We also provide financial assistance to thirty students to pay their food allowance and education fee for school, and we have provided financial assistance to another organization that helps women and children. We also gave money to all employees and teachers of one of the poorest schools in the Naser Bagh refugee camp in Peshawar, Pakistan. Through this work I had the opportunity to visit the refugees and talk to them and listen to their problems and concerns. In Kabul, I was fully covered from head to toe, and no one knew who I was, or what I was doing.

To raise money for all those projects, I buy crafts from the refugees and auction them here in Canada. The organization also gets money from membership fees, generous board members, and from personal contacts in the community. We also hold garage sales. As well, the Afghan Women's Organization also has a very successful catering business that contributes to the refugee fund.

I do not get paid for my work with the Afghan Women's Organization. To make a living, I was a settlement counselor for eight years; I helped refugees orient themselves to their new lives. Right now I do interpretation and translation work for organizations that serve refugees. These are short-term contracts and I am trying to find a job that will be flexible enough to allow me to continue my work with the Afghan Women's Organization. I also do informal consultations with people in the Afghani community on refugee law and sponsorship, but I am too embarrassed to ask for money to do this work.

The trip home to Afghanistan was my first in twenty years. I couldn't go back during the Communist regime because it

Adeena Niazi with the children enrolled in her organization's educational program, Kabul, Afghanistan, 1999.

was very risky for me. One of my colleagues in India had problems returning to India because of her relationship to me. Even though the Taliban is very aggressive to the women, there was order and peace and some sense of security on the streets. There were so many things that made me feel strange that covering my face was overshadowed. Entering my own country after twenty years — I can't explain how I felt — not being able to recognize my old neighborhood because it had been so damaged and destroyed by shelling or rockets or simply burned. My cousin asked me if I recognized the area. I did not. We went to my old house and it was collapsed. My school was destroyed. There were no familiar faces; it seemed to be a city of the dead. All I saw on the streets were men in beards and women who were totally covered. I could read the twenty years of suffering on people's faces.

I never married; I believe marriage is a choice in Islam. I was very young when I was in India, and I was completely devoted to the cause of my people and the cause of liberation. At that time I had lots of female and male friends and we worked together like brothers and sisters. I thought if I married I wouldn't have the freedom to do all this work or the time or commitment. So instead of working exclusively for myself and a small family that I

Adeena Niazi standing in front of her bedroom
in the house she saw after two decades, Kabul, Afghanistan, 1999.

would create, I decided to work for the larger society. When I announced to my friends that I would not get married, some of my close girlfriends tried to convince me that when I grew old I would regret it. But so far I have no regrets.

My mother really motivated and encouraged me. She was a brave woman and very talented. She valued education and standing on your own feet. She was one of the first Afghani women to be sent overseas for higher education under our progressive King Amanullah. But due to the mentality of those days, she had to return home and she had to marry. She wanted me to accomplish what she couldn't in her life. When I wrote and told my mother I would not marry, she was quite happy with my decision. She advised me to maintain my own culture, religion, and dignity as an Afghani Muslim woman.

I believe the work I am doing and the organization is doing is having a positive impact on the community and peoples' lives, so it is very important for me. Everyone has a goal and my goal is to be useful. A while ago I had an interview with another immigrant and refugee service organization; I was very qualified for the job and shocked when I didn't get it. I wrote the organization and asked what my weak points were. They told me they felt that the Afghan women's Organization is a part of my life, and with my current commitment to the organization, I may not be a good employee. I was hoping that my commitment would be appreciated, but I felt like it was used against me.

When I first came to Canada and took my resume — two BAs, two MAs and pre-PHD studies, university teaching and UNHCR experience — one counselor had told me I would have to start work in a factory and forget about my career. I told her I was not physically fit to work in a factory. That really disappointed me when I first came here. Although I don't use my degrees in my work, I am glad I studied Sanskrit because it gave me a greater understanding of different religions like Hinduism and Buddhism and has made me more accepting of different faiths.

Today there is no change in my lifestyle from the life I lived in Afghanistan twenty years back. I dress the same way in blazers and long skirts and pants. There was no barrier for me in Afghanistan as a woman and I was highly respected as a female teacher. My lifestyle was the same; I worked, exercised, socialized, and prayed. I still start my day with prayers and recite from the Qur'an. My faith has been a real source of strength for me.

I am also a board member of the Canadian Centre for Victims of Torture and Women in Transition (a shelter for battered women). I have been an active member of the Canadian Council for Refugees — I was on the board for four years and I am now a member of a core group on gender issues. In the past I have volunteered with the Afghan Association of Ontario, the Multicultural Coalition for Family Services, and the Refugee Law Office.

When I look back at the past two decades I am very satisfied — I did the most I could do, and I carried on with the life my mother wanted me to have. I didn't do anything that would offend my parents or my culture. I didn't align myself with a political party and supported all the parties that resisted the Soviet occupation without joining them. I worked only for humanitarian reasons. I have a lot of support from my Afghani community and from the larger Canadian community. I have received several honors and it was great to have my work

Adeena Niazi at a Mother's Day event, 1995.

acknowledged by others. When I was in Kabul, the biggest reward I got was from an orphan child. She asked me if I was going to stay with her. I said, no, her teacher would stay with her. I saw the tears in her eyes. Having a child's appreciation, that is the most rewarding thing for me.

I didn't see my father or mother after I left Afghanistan; they died of natural causes.

A close friend told me my mother said her only hope was to see me before she died. I wrote my mother and she told me she did not want me to come home just to go to jail. I had no choice but to stay away. I feel very regretful about this and it really hurts me. I also did not get to see my aunt who lived with us before she died. She was like a second mother to me. My great wish in life was to serve them.

Today my goal and dream is to go back to Afghanistan to work for the Afghani women, the refugees, and the children. I am aware of the suffering and trauma my people have experienced and I have been witness to their tears. Their cries are always with me.

Adeena Niazi